The Jesuits Driven Away from Masonry

And

Their Dagger Shattered by Freemasons

by

Nicholas de Bonneville

1788

Translated by

Eric Serejski

From Eric Serejski

- *The Chinese Kama Sutra. Sexuality and Sexual Dysfunctions in Ancient China.* Iandl, 2007
- *Le Kama Sutra chinois. Sexualité et dysfonctions sexuelles.* Iandl, 2007.
- *Shan Hai Jing. Volume 1 - The Classics of Mountains.* Iandl, 2010.

Co-Authors

- Morris, S. B.; Serejski, E. The Degree of Junior Architect. In *Freemasonry In Context: History, Ritual, Controversy.* Lexington Books, 2004.
- Morris, S. B.; Serejski, E. The Degree of Senior Architect. In *Freemasonry In Context: History, Ritual, Controversy.* Lexington Books, 2004.

Published by Eric Serejski (Innovations and Information - Iandl)

- Antoine-Ganga, Dieudonné. *Si Bacongo m'était conté.* Iandl, 2011
- Antoine-Ganga, Dieudonné. *Grand-père, parle-nous du peuple koongo.* Iandl, 2010.

The Dagger of the Jesuits found back in the Darkness

Innovations and Information, Inc. Frederick, MD

http://www.iandi.cc

ISBN 978-0-9797824-3-5

Achilles who ran without weapons to repel the whole Trojan Camp,
it is the Truth that knows how to triumph against imposture, effortless and
without cruelty."
Introduction, p. 3

Table of Content

Forward by Eric Serejski

In preparing this translation of *The Jesuits Driven Away from Masonry and Their Dagger Shattered by Freemasons*, the aim was to achieve a simple, readable text which would ring true to those who are already lovers of the complex history and allegories of Free-Masonry and would attract others to it. For this reason I have attempted to render the text into English as it is spoken today rather than the terminology that follows an exact translation of 18th century French into 18th century English. In the second place, I have made use of the familiar paragraph form, doing away as much as possible with a syntax that has significantly evolved over the last three centuries. This was done in the interest of easier reading, and in order to bring out more clearly the connection between the single statements.

No claim of literary excellence is here advanced nor any attempt to support or reject the theories of Bonneville.

The purpose of this translation is to provide an English translation of what I found to be an interesting work on the interconnections of Jesuits, Templars and Freemasons as well as supportive material in the study of the events preceding the French Revolutions. Academicians and historians of these fields my find the work of Bonneville of use. His work has generated two radical points of view: rejection or acceptance.

There are two additions to the text. I have cross-checked whenever possible all arguments and citations made by Bonneville. To his footnotes I therefore added my own while keeping them minimal. When adding them, I systematically put my comments under brackets and stated the comment with my initials, to clearly differentiate them from Bonneville's. The second addition is that of a bibliography. The bibliography includes both works cited by Bonneville and those I used to cross-check his assertions. Such biography can be of benefit as it cites interesting works in the fields of Templars, the Society of Jesus, and the Freemasons.

Introduction by Eric Serejski

Nicholas Bonneville

James Billington, the U.S. Librarian of Congress, wrote in *Fire in the Minds of Men* (1980) that "Nicolas de Bonneville" (1760-1828) of Paris was one of the "founding fathers" of the "modern revolutionary tradition." Indeed, in 1845, Karl Marx honored Bonneville's fraternal order and printing-house — the Cercle Social — as having "commenced the [modern] revolutionary movement."[1]

Nicolas de Bonneville (1760-1828) was a bookseller and printer, journalist and writer. As a young man, he produced German and English translations of the works of Jean le Rond d'Alembert, which financially supported him until his death. In particular, he was known for reproducing the essay on the origins of freemasonry by Thomas Paine, one of his close friends. Bonneville played a crucial role in the advent of Romanticism (a word first used in Bonneville's circle). He was an essential precursor of this literary movement through his own writings, inspiration and translations of major works of the German theatre of the time (*Nathan the Wise* of Lessing, the *Brigands* of Schiller, and *Goetz von Verlichingen* of Goethe).

In his late twenties, Bonneville published *The Jesuits Driven Away from Masonry and Their Dagger Shattered by Freemasons*, Paris, C. Volland, 1788, followed by *History of Modern Europe: From the Invasion of Northern Peoples in the Roman Empire until the Peace of 1783*, 3 vols. Paris, Geneva, [sn], 1789-1792 and a few years later by *Spirit of Religion: book promised and necessary to the Federal Universal Friends of Truth*, Paris, Impr. Social Circle, 1792.

In the midst of this literary production, in 1790, he founded, with Claude Fauchet, the Society of the Friends of Truth (also known as the Amis de la Vérité or the Social Club), whose purpose was to rally the human race to "the doctrine of love, which is the religion of happiness." The club became a forum for revolutionary and egalitarian ideas, attracting Sylvain Marechal and Gracchus Babeuf into his circle. It was at the time unique for its focus on social, sexual and racial equality. The Social Club was the first revolutionary group to identify itself clearly as a *cosmopolitan organization*, meaning that its aims superseded national boundaries. The reports of the Social Club were published in the newspaper, Mouth of Iron. The newspaper became

---

[1] Luchetti, Marco di. *Bonnevile's Place in History*. 2009.

one of the most sophisticated instruments of the Cordeliers Club, and it remained so until the cessation of its publication in the aftermath of the massacre on the Champ de Mars, 17 July 1791. He also published newspapers called 'The Tribune of the People', 'The Chronicle of the Month', and 'The Well Informed'. In addition to Fauchet, de Bonneville's collaborators included Louis-Sebastien Mercier, Nicolas de Condorcet, Nicolas-Edme Rétif, and Thomas Paine. In 1791, he founded the "Republican Society", whose members included Nicolas de Condorcet and Manon Roland. He was also friend and disciple to the occultist, Louis-Claude de Saint-Martin. In this short period of time, the Cercle Social created, with government funding, a daily newspaper; a monthly magazine; a separate journal for peasants and another for citydwellers; and it published about 193 books.[2]

In the aftermath of the massacre on the Champs de Mars in 1791, his publications were halted and, after denunciating the massacres of September 1792, he was arrested. Following the fall of Robespierre he was released and later jailed again for comparing Bonaparte to Cromwell and his presses were confiscated. He stayed with his friend Tom Paine in the United States for four years and then returned to France after the fall of Napoleon. During the latter years of his life, he fell into misery and madness, naturally taking a more pessimistic view on the possibilities for the happiness of mankind. His funeral expenses were paid for by Charles Nodier, Victor Hugo, and Alfred de Vigny.

Illuminati, Society of Jesus and Freemasonry

Bonneville was initiated into freemasonry in 1786 during a stay in England. In 1787, along with Savalette de Langes (head of the Paris Amis Réunis lodge), he was admitted into the Illuminati through Bod,[3] the head of the

---

[2] James H. Billington. *Fire in the Minds of Men: Origins of the Revolutionary Faith*. Basic Books, 1980.

[3] Bode, Johann Joachim Christoph (1730-1793). A bookseller in Hamburg, he was initiated into Masonry in 1791 and was of the most distinguished Masons of his time. In 1790 he joined the order of the Illuminati, obtaining the highest degree in its second class, and at the Congress of Wilhelmsbad [1782] he advocated the opinions of Weishaupt. Among many valuable contribution to Masonic literature, he translated from the French Bonneville's celebrated work entitled *Les Jésuites chasses de la Maçonnerie et leur poignard brisé par les Maçons {Die Schottische Maurerey verglichen mit den drey Ordens-Gelübden und das Geheimniss der Tempelherrn aus dem 14. Jahrhundert*, 1788}. According to Albert G. Mackey, "No man of his day was better versed than he in the history of Freemasonry, or possessed a more valuable and extensive library; no one was more diligent in increasing his stock of Masonic knowledge, or more anxious to avail himself of the rarest sources of learning." Albert G. Mackey, *Encyclopedia of Freemasonry*. 1917. P. 143.

Illuminati. It is to note that the members of this Amis Réunis lodge were all singularly the leaders of all movements in the Revolutions of 1789 and 1792.

The mid eighteenth century was stricken by an anti-Jesuit reaction that covered the entire Europe. At the time, the Illuminati sustained the theory that the Jesuits were conspiring to take over Freemasonry.[4] This movement was initiated by the Barond Adolf von Knigge (1752-1796),[5] in his *Des Jésuites, des Francs-Maçons et des Rose-Croix allemands* (1781), which borrows a lot to the Provincials of Pascal. He wrote that evidence clearly proved Jesuits infiltrated Freemasonry. He said Freemasons were obliged to use every effort to weed out this influence. But Knigge also said the Illuminati had decided to use Jesuit methods (subversion, strict discipline, etc.) to combat Jesuit objectives. He described the Illuminati Order as a counterconspiracy of enlightened men. This rhetoric backfired. It opened the door in 1786 for an Illuminatus named Ernst August of Göchhausen (1740-1824) to argue that the Illuminati themselves had been infiltrated by Jesuits. In 1788, Bonneville and Bode, who suspected that the Company of Jesus used Freemasonry for the restoration of the Stuarts on the throne of England, addressed this problem by denouncing even more loudly that the Jesuits influenced Freemasonry in Bonneville's book *Jesuits Driven Away from Masonry and their Dagger Shattered by the Masons* and its German translation by Bode. In this book, the Jesuits are accused of having introduced into the symbolic degrees of freemasonry, the myths of the Templars and their doctrine of revenge, based on the "crime" of their

---

[4] A detailed analysis of the role of the Illuminati and of Bonneville and their putative role in the French revolution can be found in the unpublished work of Marco di Luchetti on the Illuminati of Bavaria and on his translation of Bonneville l'*Esprit des religions*
(http://sites.google.com/site/illuminatiofbavaria/ visited February 2011)
[5] Knigge, Adolph F. R. L. (1752-1796) - German Freemason and, in part, founder of the Bavarian Illuminati. He was initiated in a lodge of the Strict Observance at Cassel in 1772, he became one of the foremost German writers on the subject. He published *Avertissement aux princes allemands, pour les mettre en garde contre l'esprit et le poignard des Jésuites {A Warning to the German Princes to guard against the spirit and dagger of the Jesuits}, On The Jesuits, Freemasons and the German Rosicrucians {Ueber Jesuiten, Freymauer und deutsche Rosencreutzer}*, 1781, anon.; *Essay on Freemasonry {uber die Friemaurerei}*, 1784; *Contribution towards the latest history of the Order of Freemasons {Beytrag zur neusten Geschiket}*, 1786; and *Philo's final Declaration*, 1788. He also wrote many non-Masonic works, one being *On Conversation with Men*, towards the end of his career and after a sad experience with the Illuminati and disappointment with the Strict Observance, causing him therein to devote much space to secret societies and denunciation of Freemasonry. The most interesting and significant part of Knigge's career was his participation with Weishaupt in the promotion of the Bavarian Illuminati, he being almost an equal party. See also Mackey, pp. 521-522.

destruction, and the four vows of the Templars included in their higher degrees.

Bonneville's work and role in the multifactorial inducers of the French revolution and in the inter-relationships between Jesuits, Freemasonry and Illuminati have remained relatively unknown. It is interesting that his *Les Jésuites chassés* has been reproduced entirely in the monumental *Histoire des religions et des moeurs de tous les peoples du monde*, Volume 6, 1818 (Augmented Edition). This work, referred to as *The Book That Changed Europe* by Hunt et al.,[6] was to become the groundwork for religious tolerance.

To cite the Editor of the section on Freemasonry of this work,

> "The historical observations and research of the author of the work titled *Les Jésuites chassés de la Franc-Maçonnerie, et leur poignard brisé par les Maçons, et la Maçonnerie écossaise comparée avec l'ordre des Templiers du quatorzième siècle* appeared to us of an interest worthy of being included in this volume, as masonic conclusion. The praises of Mirabeau and the confessions of Mallet du-Pan in the *Mercure de France* of 1788, and those of one of the German translators easily identified as one of the heads of the Highest Masonry, prove the merit of the work, for which no writer has dared answer for the last thirty years, and where the true Masons go to seek the Ariadne's thread to help them walk in this inextricable labyrinth.[7]

---

[6] See Hunt, Lynn, Margaret C. Jacob, and Wijnand Mijnhardt. *The Book That Changed Europe: Picart and Bernard's "Religious Ceremonies of the World"* (Harvard University Press; 383 pages; 2010).
[7] *Histoire des religions et des moeurs de tous les peoples du monde*, Volume 6, 1818, p. 132. The editor also adds, p. 188, that "there have been several translations of this work in Germany; the most respected one, enriched with notes, is attributed to the Grand Master of the Templars: he describes in his well-written preface that, without warranting the truth or the probability of a strange discovery, he only dared translating the work of Nicolas de Bonneville by remaining anonymous.

1. Scottish Masonry Compared With the Three Vows and the Secret of Templars of the 14th Century.

Orient of London

1788

To the Dearest
And most respectable lodge
of the Réunion des Étrangers,
ORIENT DE PARIS,
This General and Complete
History
of the
Triumph of Freemasonry
Is
very Fraternally
Dedicated

Orient of London
1788

By Nicolas de Bonneville

Introduction

καὶ τόνδ' ἔσῳζον οἶκον ἐς τόδ' ἡμέρας.

ὁσίου γὰρ ἀνδρὸς ὅσιος ὢν ἐτύγχανον.
Apollo. Euripide. Alcesti.

Up to now, I have been the protector of this house,
Because it was of a Holy Man the Holy House
The Sun-God, in Alcestis by Euripides

For the last few years the main goal of a chosen society has been to gather and collect the whole spirit of the centuries. However it does not yet have historians that it can recognize. It has no annals whose straight and free language would precisely mean what it says: It is up to the experts to conclude if the task is possible. Bacon was of yesterday, he was the minister of free people, and yet he barely dared shed some lights on the history of the human mind.

"The one who has a nose for it will pick it up" said Montaigne or someone else. My purpose is not to write here the history of this society: ten generations of men would not be enough for such a task. My purpose is to teach the philosopher to respect a large society, already including more than twenty millions of men, all selectively admitted. I will only write with simplicity the history of its triumph over the *invisible* hands that were equipped with hope, scepters and daggers for about a century.

Like the good Plutarch, I do not want being thought of as more knowledgeable or better than I am. I like to say publically that some foreign literates have provided me precious research and important legal documents in their languages (I am especially grateful to the very dear and very respectable loge de la Réunion des Étrangers). The small part that I may have in these *historical essays* is to see them linked in a book nourished by my studies, my ideas and my purposes.

Probably the discovery new underground politics, still incomprehensible for so many years of patience to tireless observers, will shed a major light on the history of the upheavals of our modern Europe; it will be a major benefit for our Europe because the more we waive the light of reason, the more the attention of people wakes up, and they learn to look far away and to see around them.

1. Scottish Masonry and Templars

Let there be light! Let us pull up a side of the respectful veil behind which some jugglers and schemers cheer one another and lead numerous people blindly and who are truly the elite of our Europe.

However we cherish a human and generous government: we are also among these good people spoken about by Saint Augustine, who persecute bad people only with a wise discretion, and who like surgeons full of humanity consider carefully what they cut instead of not looking where to strike like murders do. When the NAZARENE wanted to purify the Holy Temple, he did not carry swords and flames; he only armed himself with a *whip* to drive out the bandits that desecrated the Holy of Holies by an infamous traffic. Achilles ran without weapons to drive out the whole camp of Troy. It is the TRUTH that triumphs over imposture without effort and without cruelty.

Scottish Masonry and the Templar Order

Would this still be the time when our weak sight cannot be lightened by being to close from the light of the tradition? Should we still need to rely on the invisible hands of the Eternal? Could it therefore be possible that without immediately going down from Heaven a fortunate institution produces learned legislators, heroes and men? Some god-men, the true images of a God on earth! A Society needs to be recommendable through its great purposes and through the enlightened devotion of its constituting members; but it matters little that is was created yesterday, or that its origin, even recognized, is of time immemorial. A society that glorifies itself to be ancient has some good resemblance with these families that were illustrious and that were compared by Bacon, if I am not wrong, to old castles. Then, to the eyes of the sage, would an edifice be honored through its founder or through its owner? However, I must admit, the sensible traveler stops, with his heart moved with emotion, in front of these august monuments. Monuments that time takes pleasure, in its vanity, to erase everywhere the hand of men, and has somehow animated under the embraces of vigorous ivy whose thick and silvery hair witnesses its endless strength, and an uncertain birth that seems to touch to creation. He contemplates in his soft mediations the old surrounding wall of an antique vault that appears to him overloaded by the weight of accumulating centuries He meditates for the celestial pleasures of inspiration. However if suddenly he meets the confabulation of hypocrites, impure reptiles, or tigers or brigands, or a stupid heir, no matter his respect for the building he is admiring, and for the great men that have sanctified it by their presence, he dares not look at it anymore: dragging his sight in the dust, he goes hastily away from a desecrated sanctuary.

It is not without a major purpose that numerous writers brought the origin of Freemasonry to the highest antiquity. Benefiting from some shadows of the expert allegories of Pythagoras, of Semonides, of Homer and Pindar, it was easy to force the learned mind, avid of learning, to perpetual searches, without ever becoming discouraged by unsuccessful late nights. He is certain that there are cults so absurd that they could never enter without reason in the mind of the sages of a century, not even go out of them, no matter along times the delirium of the human mind. So, he searches in all monstrous allegories a natural meaning that satisfies him. Far from ridiculing the most bizarre ceremonies, he submits them to his reason, with respect, to keep these allegories intact and pure. He looks at these allegories as a veil drawn between the lost history and the one that remains to us. He analyzes them and gathers them like the fragments of a persecuted truth. A study that made him an observer, that taught him to think, that showed him the whole importance of perfecting oneself in the art of *seeking for oneself*; this study agrees to him, consoles him, he delights in it. It is truly him who is attentive to isolated and luminous facts that without presenting anything else but simple glimmers announce clarities.[8] What is already proven pure for the thinking man, but which is a sublime discovery for the child who has never deepened anything, renders him respectful up to enthusiasm for the conservation of an allegoric ceremony from which he draws a literal meaning that he finds simple and reasonable: he likes the innocent subterfuge of the allegories that protect the truth against the furors of the superstition altered by the blood of his brother. No matter the explanation someone gives to him, he searches in it *his own* in these multi-facets mirrors that the talented person was compelled to use to abuse the wicked and indiscreet people.

Therefore, the sages have a *motivated* respect for the *ancient* allegories. Now, if it is true that the Philosopher respects an allegory that he cannot explain, one must nevertheless prove to him that it is *ancient*; that he *sees* it as respectable and dear to the men whose irreproachable conduct announces a straight and perceptive meaning. He would not resemble those so-called strong-minded people who despise all that they do not understand, he always suspect a reason, nothing rebuts him, and as soon as he stop seeing the antique trace, he is even more in a rush to discover the hidden hand that acts in silence. He sees the ridicule ribbons and some secret on sale as despicable monopoles. I don't know but it seems that the heart of an honest man always has a secret voice that reveals to him through a painful shout the invisible presence of the crime, and there may be a benevolent God who does not always permit that virtue remains forever on earth without reward.

The society of freemasons has had, throughout times and in various parts of the world where it flourished and still flourishes, members full of the rarest knowledge and of an unquestionable merit. Probably satisfied that what they found conformed to the ancient allegories, they focused with less hurry to raise other veils that they may found modern or at least altered by negligence or stupidity. Since they felt that politics entered in no ways in the Jovian, magical, Celtic, or Egyptian allegories, they offered no resistance to

---

[8] See Bacon on mythology [SE: Probably his preface of *The Wisdom of the Ancients*].

imperceptible innovations unknown to them and called new grades by the ancients of the order. The allegorical system of the first benefactors of the human kind was disfigured progressively. It was replaced by a degrading and cruel system adopted under the emblem of the mysterious style of the annals of the ancient world.

Indeed, instead of the obscure allegories whose antiquity at least led to think, millions of men were led to accept the hope of deserving the explanation of a bunch of important mysteries of which the key, as it was said, was between the hands of the Supérieurs Inconnus S.I.[9] Those who relied on some ancient philosophers have taken in good faith the numbers and computations of their infernal machinations for the numbers of Pythagoras, whose perfect knowledge was a deep science of the mysteries of nature according to Pythagoras' disciples.

Since one already needs to think a lot to discern what is reasonable when studying the mysteries of nature, and since one looses his mind and heart when trying to untangle the mysteries of the wicked, I must provide some details that may bring to a larger number of people a very important idea about me. Allow me therefore, to be better understood, to compare nature to a thinking being who works publically and in open light, but always by modesty, or caprice, or by a law unknown to me, covered with a more or less thick veil. If I enter in its atelier, and if I pay careful attention to its movements full of grace; if I hear a caressing voice, I already know that it is not a tiger hidden under the veil. I would suspect a skilled artist or a learned woman; it may be a young woman born for love: through lucky negligence or kindness of her heart, she may uncover part of the veil. I might learn about her beauty: maybe by the study of her features seized surreptitiously, I would be able to untangle the true path to her heart and then learn from her mouth her origin and the reason of the impenetrable veil that hides her divine features and her creative hand. I want her to appear one moment insensitive to my prayer: at least I might know the purpose of my research. After having obtained a lot, would I not want even more? Then, if necessity would not allow me to stay in contemplation much longer in the workshop, how happy might I find myself meditating with the great men of our century, to learn from them the history of all the cues that the Supérieur Inconnu, under the veil, might have given of the procedures of his work, or of the mystery of his gender! And if they respected the truth enough and a rather good impression about my zeal to offer me *witnesses* and not interpretations, how much gratitude and happiness I would owe them! But if some *man of secrets* would invite me to his trust, if he would show me to his house on fixed days, and if I always had a new domestic personnel to solicit, another door to open; if the grand master is always absent, if some wannabe initiated persons contradict one another in what they say about the marvels and purposes of

---

[9] [SE: Supérieur Inconnu, or Unknown Superior. Since Bonneville uses the initials S.I. in some of his analyses, I will use the French expression throughout the book.]

their superior; if they cannot even teach me the name or the nature of the inaccessible Proteus, I would shout while shivering: "Nothing is good here"!

Those various feelings are more or less what we meet today in Freemasonry; a holly respect for ancient allegories; and the indignation for the *enigmas* that are suspected to be – rightfully – quite modern. Someone said that the truth was more valuable to humanity than the one who found it. I think so! Let us shed an eternal light on the bloody scoundrels who, armed with daggers, slide in the celebrations of nature and friendship, who speak of revenge; making the temple of goodness and truth become only a cavern of scoundrels and imposters; this august temple that has never been closed but to fanatics who get irritated at everything without knowing why, and especially at the truth, which, always useful to the human kind, has never hurt except those who lure men.[10]

A complete history of the society of the Freemasons, confirmed by authentic monuments, is the only method we thought of adopting, as the simplest one, to set honest people right, who are led to murder and slavery by always being spoken about independence, about innocent games, and about beneficence and *equality*. In this way, the pontiffs, when they were still small bishops without power in Rome, were speaking of a *brotherhood* of a community of goods; but always with a *blind* obedience to the orders of the Eternal of whom they said with humility being the representatives. As soon as they *armed* their brothers to avenge the *cause of a God spoiled by blood*, they were seen only as monsters of cruelty. The kings, for whom they first pretended to consolidate the authority, were required to kneel in front of them. One would see a pope, Adrian IV, dictate his will to the sovereign of a great kingdom where his father and himself had begged. They made states, tributes, and homage bestowed onto them. And in reward, they gave to the powerful usurer crowns *to conquest*, up to seas that did not belong to them. Finally by dint of persuading Sovereigns, capable to resist them, to not refuse themselves to acts of *Christian humility that was demanded from kings by an ancient custom*, they subjected them little by little to the disgraceful homage of a perpetual vassalage. Henry II, Frederick I *Barbarossa*, Philippe *Augustus*, and many more other monarchs and emperors of untamed courage learned, but too late, that the king who roots a mistake in his kingdom, would often be forced to devour the bitterness of it. They were offended in vain by the insolence of the pontiffs; the pontiffs always triumphed. They called without shame their episcopal chair *the throne of the sovereign of sovereigns* of the earth! And those who served them, their *brethren*, their *allied*, their *equals*, whom they had temporarily *subjected* to a *real* obedience, under the august oath, and renewed daily, to lavish them with glory and unexpected wealth, were dispossessed, despised, and chained! They claimed in vain oaths and *their tittles!* What are the most legitimate titles when the ambitious one, having the authority on his side,

---

[10] See the Preface of Boulanger's *Christianity Unveiled*. [SE: English Translated by W. M. Johnson, 1835].

makes his evil genius an ALMIGHTY, and when he announces to the frightened nations bloody orders from a peaceful God, who never had a language other than the holly laws of nature?

The Jesuits were the first ones to give a history to Freemasonry, as soon as they succeeded to make of it a complete allegory of the various degrees of their order. First they first published it as unsubstantiated. They said it was inconsequential and the work of ignorance and greed. This was about eliminating, through clever politics, the keen investigation of a merciless observer. However, as this history aged, the eye of censure was not to be feared anymore: it was too tired of new extravagances to look again at something thrown away, and to do an in-depth examination. Therefore, they stared progressively to acknowledge its authenticity. Who is the man knowledgeable enough of the details of the general history, to know with precision the dates of such or such event of the past centuries? It is quite feasible that a king had a brother, it was said and it was believed, nobody suspected something strange in a plethora of similar assertions. It is so hard to examine, and so painful to suspect imposture. Therefore history has been falsified without measure to fool millions of men who, for centuries, became accustomed to believe blindly. Moreover, the elementary and abridged histories are generally the only one that one reads quickly and also quite rarely. They are also insufficient to provide an ordinary person the ability to rectify dates and to verify frivolous assertions. What happened to this negligence of criticizing the first histories of the masonic society of the Jesuits? It is because they dared attesting as authentic, through the solemnity of a judicial oath, an impertinent history that offers at best weak relationships with the annals of our most serious historians.

When we start reflecting upon this, with this strange history at hand, and when we discover one after the other the lie and the truth, we fall wounded in an *unfathomable* chaos. There are few observers who feel how such a mistake fed in the shadows can be one day fatal to the human kind. Still, it often happens that an intelligent man, who always has for causes the happiness of his country and the universal peace, cannot waste long years in uncertain attempts according to feelings.

The Jesuits, who always wanted that their conspirators to follow a celibate life to give no hostages to fortune, appear to have taken into account all the obstacles of a serious research, not thinking it would be possible. It is tempting to think that the *unknown superiors* would question one another on the suspicions that they could have created about the hidden goal of the Jesuitic Masonry, and that each one then worked at eliminating the clues that could lead to a discovery. Because one has seen all their efforts to annihilate public acts and careless works that escaped their attention in the intoxication of their success: Masonry *analyzed* by S. Pritchard. This book had 21 editions in England and there is no available public copy of it today, regardless of the amount offered to a Bookstore. The Jesuits were quite embarrassed: It was necessary to speak about the society in order to *sing of arms and of a man;*[11] and they had to fear creating the smallest spark. But the spark was found and tended; it was covered under the ashes and one may ask with impatience where the powder magazine is!

The erudition of some modern Mason is accurate and deep: the charlatanism of the jugglers sent by the S.I. as recruiters led to numerous polemic writings, to the shame of the mysterious grand order. Suddenly a book emerged whose judicious critic and infinite research deserved the esteem of all scholars in Germany: I speak here about an essay on the order of the Templars by C. F. Nicolaï.[12] Shouldn't such work be written with the stylistic elegance and amicable graces that bring all European classes of citizens to read our charming bagatelles?

The remarkable essay of the learned Nicolaï on the order of the Templars helped me greatly to link interesting facts and to analyze them up to the evidence. This was a faint gleam, but a true beam of light: following the example of this deep philosopher, I tried to substitute to the method of teaching so easy and so common to our witty critics, the thorough analytic method rarely found today in France but in the works of Charles Bonnet, Condorcet and Bailly.

I only beg attention from all friends of humanity in order to grasp the probabilities that will result from the rigorous examination of a large number of facts. Indeed, it is not the conjectures that result from *facts*; it is always a perfect image of the *features and character* of a hidden truth. Then the mere connection between them suffices to render the truth known in its totality. In this way, in the shadows we could suspect the return of a missing friend by the remote sound of his steps; and we would not doubt his arrival upon hearing his voice.

The captain George Smith, who must not be confused, despite his celebrity, with Adams Smith, author of a renowned work on the wealth of nations, printed a so-called history of the origin and the antiquity of Freemasonry in London.

In this history, everything seems innocent, puerile and almost without aims. While it is not a model of elegance and precision, it is a masterpiece of tricks

---

[11] *Arma virumque cano.* This is the slogan of the patents of the Grand Order G.O. [SE: Quote from Virgil's Aeneid.]

[12] [SE: Christoph Friedrich Nicolaï (1733-1811), *Versuch über die Besschuldigungen welch dem Tempelherrnorden gemacht worden und über dessen Geheimniss; nebst einem Anhange uber das Entstehen der Freimaurergesellschaft* (An Essay on the accusations made against the Order of Knights Templar and their mystery; with an Appendix on the origin of the Fraternity of Freemasons), Berlin: 1782. Albert Mackey says of him, "Few will be found at the present day to concur in all his views, yet none can refuse to award to him the praise of independence of opinion, originality of thought, and an entire avoidance of the beaten paths of hearsay testimony and unsupported tradition. His results may be rejected, but his methods of attaining them must be commended."]

and intrigues. The apparent and quite frequent contradictions should not rebuke the reader: as soon as we gain possession of a Jesuit master key, we see that a same purpose always link these contradictions. This includes the titles of their works. They have a hidden meaning under very common words that, in themselves, also offer a clear meaning to the tasteful reader: he does not suspect that a title has much importance. Indeed, who would ever break his head digging through a book whose bizarre title does not give its true concept?

The incredible success of this work among Freemasons is a painful proof that even in our century that people can fall under the spell of any charlatan, and easily believe. This does not render a great homage to the human mind. I will highlight for the reader some curious articles of the work of Mr. the Captain George Smith, Inspector of the *Royal Military Academy at Woolwich, Provincial, Provincial Grand Master for the county of Kent, and R.A.*

It has for title *The Use and Abuse of Free-Masonry*. It does not mean, although this is easy to imagine, "Use and Abuse of Freemasonry", but Use - U - or 20, and Abuse – A – or 1. Now 1 and 20 give 21 or V. The first result is therefore V.V. or *Venerandus, Venerandi*. This title designates the *clergy* in general.

For fear of confusing my reader from the beginning of these computations, they will be presented a second time. Before reaching the end of my book, the reader will be quite capable to find the accomplishment of the four Jesuit Vows in the *Free-Masonry* words.

The Use and Abuse of Masonry appears to me a rather inadequate title for the work of Mr. Smith, especially since the words *use and abuse* have a revolting cacophony in the English language: but I *evidently* see that I was by a hasty judgment: I agree that its true title, the *Jesuit Clergy*, has an immediate relationship with all the paragraphs of his *double-sided* book.

"Freemasons" continues Mr. George Smith, "are *well informed* from their own private and interior records, that the building of Solomon's temple, *S.T.*, is an important era, from whence we derive many mysteries of our art. Now, be it remembered, that this great event took place above a thousand years before the Christian era; and consequently more than a century before Homer, the first of the Grecian poets, wrote; [13] and above five centuries before Pythagoras brought from the East his system of *truly masonic* instruction, to *illuminate* the Western World.

But, remote as is this period, we date not from thence the commencement of our art; for though it might owe to the wise and glorious king some of its many mystic forms and hieroglyphic

---

[13] *The Use and Abuse of Free-Masonry*. London, Kearfley, No 46, 1783, page 21. [SE - The edition used here is the New York: Masonic Publishing and Manufacturing Co. 1866. Page 10].

ceremonies, yet certainly the art itself is coeval with man, its great object of it." [14]

As Mr. Smith states, it is likely that the society, of which *he mentions being an enlightened member*, has secret annals attesting its origin, its principles and the purposes. However, it must not be believed, as he tries to make us hear it, that the sublime Art, called *Free* and *Accepted* Masonry by him, is of a solemn antiquity. The Mysteries of the enlightened society of Mr. Smith were certainly not transmitted by Adam to Methuselah and then to Noah.

Society-S – Illuminati -I. -S.-I - Societas Jesuitarum.

Today, the Jesuits, preened by several centuries of success, handle with a lot of contempt these last remains of the druids in Europe, and have *masoned* them to their *politics*.

Mr. Smith does assert that the most *perfect remains* of the Druid rituals and ceremonies are *preserved* (beware of this word *preserved*) in the customs and ceremonies of Masons. [15]

The original names of Masons and Masonry may *probably* be derived from, or *corrupted* from, said Mr. Smith, who is so well educated on the secret history of the society, the Greek words *mysterion, res arcana*, mysteries, and *myres, sacris initiatus mysta*, those initiated in the sacred mysteries. [16]
The Greek words used by Mr. Smith; impose on those who don't know this language, and the number unfortunately for the art to write is quite large. If he had written in his scholarly etymologies in Latin characters, could he have made us suspect some analogy between the words *mysterion* and *Free and Accepted Masonry*?
The etymological science of Mr. Smith is even incredible because he writes some sentences earlier:

"It seems as if the name of Masons was compounded of *Maô-Zôan, quaero Salutem* [I look for the Salute]; and the title Masonry no more than a corruption, of *Mesouraneô, sum in medio coeli* [I am in the midst of Heaven], or *Mazouzooth, signa coelestia, celestial signs*; which conjectures are strengthened by our symbols. [17]

---

[14] *Idem*, page 11.
[15] Smith, G. I am bold to assert the most perfect remains of the Druids rites and ceremonies are preserved in the customs and ceremonies of Masons. P. 16-17.
[16] Smith, G. Page 17. [SE: Smith's terms are Μυστήριον and Μύρησ.]
[17] Smith, G. Page 16. [SE: Smith's terms are Μαω-Σωαν, Μεσιυρανεω, and Μαζουνοοθ (*Mazzaroth*).]

These are many doubts about a writer as knowledgeable as Mr. Smith says being in the history of his society; but he needed a Greek word; and of a Greek word found in a translation of the book of Job and the Genesis.[18]

Still, Mr. Smith humbly presumes that the name of Freemason does not indicate that - *This society was originally composed of builders and public architects*!

> "There's always leakage of deceit. Which makes it never safe to cheat."[19]

According to Mr. Smith,

> "For at the time in which Moses ordained the setting up of a sanctuary, and King Solomon a Temple, "dedicated to the Lord, to the *King* of the Kings", that the most recommendable men to conduct the works were selected. It was on those occasions that our predecessors appeared to the world as architects; ... since which period *builders* have adopted the name of Masons."[20]

It seems to me that we need a rather jesuitic trust to not fear that such absurdities, when presented solemnly to thousands of people, make them open at least one eye on their intrigues.

How is that! There would be a secret history of the origin of the society, and one would give such impertinences to devour? And to obtain the revelation of the *mysteries* of this enlightened society, we would suffer having leaders who are, like at the time of the birth of the world, false Gods; who only become visible by their cruelty, their insolence and their greed. Then, we would patiently allow these generals to say that they are Masons by excellence while hiding themselves from the whole society of Masons; allow that they feed from feeble minds in the delirium of fanaticism and of ridiculous expectations, capable to arm a brother against his brother; allow that they drown in blood entire nations; and allow that they renew these horrible crusades that under the pretext of arguing a tomb opened an abyss to bury Europe and Asia!

> "Methuselah who died but a few days before the general deluge lived 245 years with Adam, by whom he was instructed in all the mysteries of this sublime science, which he faithfully communicated to his grandson Noah, who transmitted it to posterity: and since this

---

[18] Book of Job, 38:32. Exodus 2:46.

[19] [SE: La Fontaine - The Wolf Turned Shepherd].

[20] Smith, G. P. 16 [SE: the exact quote is "for at the time in which Moses ordained the setting up of a sanctuary, and when Solomon was about to build the Temple of Jerusalem, they selected from out of the people, those men who ... were found proper to conduct these works of piety"]

> *mysterious* knowledge has always been kept with the whole reverence and prudence that such a precious treasure deserved, being always confined to a *small number* of elected."[21]

If I were to continue in the details of these allegories, I would depart too much from my more important analyses. Let us only observe here that in the holy chronology Methuselah lived with Adam only 243 years. I must also warn that this change could not really be a typographic mistake. Let's not stop to trifles: *pauperis is numerare pecus* [leave it to the *poor* to count their flocks].

> "... every nation having had *some share* in their propagation; but according to their *different* manners, some have cultivated them with more accuracy, perseverance, and success than others: and though the secrets of the *royal art* have not been indiscriminately revealed, they have nevertheless been communicated in every age to such as were worthy to receive them."
> "But I am not at liberty publicly to undraw the curtain, and openly to descant on this head; it is [a] sacred [repository], and ever will remain so: those who are honored with the trust [to be admitted to the Sanctuary] will not reveal [the sacred mysteries], except to the truly qualified *brother*, and they who are ignorant of it cannot betray it."[22]

> "For as all things in process of time are liable to decay and corruption, the ancient professors wisely foreseeing the great abuses which heir exalted mysteries might sustain, if *generally* made known, determined to confine the knowledge of them only to select brethren, *men* whom they had found by *long* experience to be well versed in the general principles of the *society*, ..."
> Hence it is that a man may be sufficiently able to acquit himself in every test that is laid down by our present institution, to prove his regular initiation therein, [and also] to show that he is not unacquainted with its general principles, and yet at the same time he may be totally ignorant and undeserving of the more valuable parts of this ancient society..."
> ..."It is not every one that is barely initiated into Freemasonry, that is entrusted with all the mysteries thereto belonging; they are not attainable as things of course, nor by every capacity."[23]

---

[21] Smith, G. [SE: and it has ever been preserved with a veneration and prudence suitable to its great importance, being always confined to the knowledge of the worthy only, or ought so to be.] p. 12.

[22] Smith, G. Pp. 12-13.

[23] Smith, G. P. 13.

So many honest people are deceived! They are going to become initiated into mysteries that one tells them to be august, and they will always be the only ones excluded from them. It is said that the letter -G- in the blazing star is the biggest secret of Freemasonry, and it will never be explained in the lodges. However this mystery is entrusted to privileged beings. *A privileged society out of the society exists therefore!*

The contradictions of these historians of the mysteries do not awaken the suspicions of a society that count its members by thousands! This is what is extraordinary. The principles of this mysterious knowledge that the Almighty entrusted to Adam; says Mr. Smith, have been until us inviolably concealed and keenly propagated. Next he speaks of the construction of Salomon's temple, as of another period to which the society owes a big part of its inappreciable secrets. On the other hand, Samuel Pritchard places the first origin of the Royal Art to the construction of the tower of Babel: he assures that the secrets of this Art were communicated by Euclid; an Egyptian philosopher, to Hiram, the architect of Salomon's temple. May they reconcile with one another, these worthy elected, initiated in the major Mysteries of Free and Accepted Masonry!

Let's quickly say: the contradictions of the historian adepts are only in appearance, and we will know how to reconcile them. As a friend of history a historian, who must be only a historian, can be delighted with an unexpected discovery that brings him major clarification on falsified facts: but as a member of the society, whose supposed chiefs publish a forged history; is it possible not to be indignant at the sight of their impostures prepared for murders!

Mr. Smith assures that the members of the society of the Free and Accepted Masonry confess themselves to be Christians, and that he cannot really understand how the Jews, the Persians and the Turks hasten to associate themselves to it, and that nevertheless he knows several of them to be excellent Masons. In the Masonic *Book of Constitutions*, printed for the first time in London in 1723, a recipient is required be of the religion "in which all men agree," and further, on page 54, the *Catholic* religion is expressly named: and on page 50, Masonry is specified as a point of reunion for all religions.

I would be happy if I could indicate the natural source of all these contradictions, of all these incomprehensible *mysteries*, because definitely those initiated in them won't betray it.

First it is demonstrated that the histories of Free and Accepted Masonry suppose the *existence* of some unknown men who have a sacred repository in their hands; that these men have the right to exclude from their secrets whoever causes them offense, and that in this way their mysteries are always hidden from *natives*.

The existence of these *invisible* men is the central point from where is a *circle of light* will leave and highlight what is hidden in the symbolic chaos of the innovations of Masonry. Then, we will see a project set to propagate some mistakes, always tragic; and to enslave reason. A little bit of attention, and I will be clear for everybody.

In France, in Italy, in Germany, and especially in Russia, one cherishes the hope to be admitted one day to miraculous secrets by *beneficent* superiors who watch over all members of the society. We find a large number of sensical there. All of them say that if the Masonic assemblies didn't have *hope* as a purpose, it would have stopped existing long ago; and after fifteen or twenty years of useless trials, they wait, without whispering, for the unknown balm!

This idea is not as prevalent in England. This country of trading people uses its sparse leisure time only in perfecting its factories and its foreign inventions. In Masonry, an Englishman only looks for the links that will be useful in his journeys: it is a formidable association of which he is a very proud member, because he is assured every day that it is ancient. Naturally vain, he participates in fooling himself; so long as his pride is flattered, it pays. The trials *entertain* him, because they often have in his hands something cruel enough, In addition, as part of a thinking people, he finds it wiser to drink to the health of Masons rather then exposing himself elsewhere to lose his money and his health to all sorts of gambling games.

They like pump and great ceremonies in their assemblies: they come out of their ateliers with their ribbons, their shields, their flags, and their golden Bible, to render public honors to the memory of their dignitary brethren. They inaugurated publicly a lodge whose first expenses already went over twelve thousand Louis: They like the looks of a public astonished by the Masonic attire so much that they repeated the ceremony various times. I don't know what petition they presented three times to the parliament to add more to the public respect of which they are covetous. These English Freemasons are generally some honest people. However some of them suspect being led by the tip of the nose; but they are few.

The Freemasons gathered at the mother-lodge under the *Mallet* of the duke of Cumberland, brother of the King, offered me a charming spectacle: I found there a brotherly order and an imposing majesty of which the parliament of England had not given me the idea. When the duke of Cumberland announced the initiation of the Prince of Wales,[24] who was not yet far enough advanced in rank to enter in a lodge of Perfect Masonry,[25] I saw the birth of a

---

[24] [SE: The Prince of Wales was made a Mason on February 6, 1787, at an occasional Lodge convened for the purpose at the Star and Garter tavern, Pall Mall, over which the Duke of Cumberland presided. See Preston, W. *Illustrations of Masonry.* 1829, for a discussion of the history of Freemasonry in England during that period.]

[25] [SE: The term perfect Masonry is found used in some documents pertaining to the Rite of Seven Degrees in London. See Draffen, G. *Some Further Notes on the Rite of Seven Degrees in London. Ars Quatuor Coronatorum* 68 (1956): 95.]

patriotic enthusiasm, and also of major expectations. I am certain that these expectations will not suffer disappointment. The Prince of Wales is too noble and too generous to ever permit that the snake escaped from the friends of humanity warms itself under the beams of its glory, and that inspecting with its poisons any unfortunate who is not on the guards, it triumphs, with complaisance, in the Ile de la Liberté.[26]

The English Freemasons, by their charity, by their encouragements given to the industry, provide the highest honor to the society. However, more than everywhere else and from time to time, some of its members renew the idea of the Superior Inconnus; and one suffers from it. Is this tolerance? No! It is lack of concern, ignorance, and blindness! It is a crime to pay no attention to men armed with daggers who *preach* some Superior Inconnus; it is to expose the English constitution to a serious threat. I don't see this as a very pressing [issue] today; but a little more indifference, and there won't be a remedy anymore. An Englishman must only cherish liberty and not license:[27] Scottish Master, answer me: If you want the laws of your homeland to be respected, who armed you in the shadows? You are free! You say? Then, what do you want to do with a dagger?

Finally, the Superior Inconnus have succeeded so well in linking the society of the Free and Accepted Masons to the extinguished Templar order, that today there may not be one perfect Master who would dare doubt this connection. It is therefore not surprising that the grade of Templar is highly worshiped in jesuitic Masonry. In Germany it is performed with the most august solemnity. In the English lodges that are slightly *illuminated* - I – [enlightened], in other words, jesuitized, it is not tolerated that a Templar pays his dues at the banquet. The situation is not totally the same in France: *generally*, the French people consider Masonry as an institution of beneficence and as an honest gathering for feasts and games. They don't recognize a title of honor that exempts from expenses of the brotherly banquet. This cost is also not as reasonable as it is in England. In England the goal is not the banquet. In France, *a large number of lodges* consider the banquet as the main goal and there has to be a protection against parasitic visitors. The number of these visitors would soon increase in lodges if the high ranks, granted so easily there, were a title of admission to the banquet: the purpose of the enormity of the dues was probably to drive all sorts of people away from a chosen assembly.

It seems to me that in itself it is not important to believe or not to believe that the society of the Freemasons is only the order of the Templars escaped

---

[26] [SE: *Isle de la Liberté*. (1) Island of Oleron or (2) Ile de la Liberté, an island in the Pays de la Loire.]

[27] [SE: Liberty vs license. See Rousseau, Kant and Locke. "We might, over and above all this, add, to what man acquires in the civil state, moral liberty, which alone makes him truly master of himself; for the mere impulse of appetite is slavery, while obedience to a law which we prescribe to ourselves is liberty." Rousseau, *The Social Contract*.]

from the persecutions and the stakes. *Honest people* can keep this belief as it does not harm the public interests. Now Masonry still has no serious historians and its history has still not been intertwined with that of the opinions and the human mind. Definitely this jesuitic assertion ought to be proven as Masonry deserves to have historians worthy of the respects of the scholarly Europe like a David Hume, a Muller, another Tacit, and another Boulanger.

Our French writers disregard too much the philosophical analysis of the old and modern languages whose knowledge is *necessary* to write the history of the mistakes of the human mind. Among us, a Boulanger is a phenomenon. This study is however the only one that can lead to understand the root of prejudices. Rousseau himself felt it so well that he mentioned his weak attempt on the topic, a few pages long, as the most useful of his works.

A quick look on Free and Accepted Masonry shows me that it has a significant influence on the customs of our Europe, on the reigning opinions; and on the indestructibility of some mistakes always propagated. [I mean by that] that the great writers who attacked them directly in the heavens, as already not holding anymore to the earth, did not suspected at all that within darkness these same mistakes that they believed old were cherished. These mistakes were used to root fanaticism, feeding it with mysteries and expectations; once more submitting the rights of reason to *unmarried* priests who identify with the Divinity. [These are the priests] whose ferocious and cruel decisions are divine oracles. [These are the priests] who make poor craftsmen, already burdened by taxes, buy ridiculous titles. [These are the priests] who dare gather men-children to tell them: "I will make a gift to you one day, if I feel like it. In the meanwhile, adore me, and prepare weapons and soldiers for me. Sovereigns, bow down before me, and I will give you an iron rod again."

Such was in every century the language of the ambitious priest, the language of the *impure mind*: "If you *adore* me, all these things will be yours". "*I will give*" you (and not I give you) *all these things, if while bowing down to your feet, you adore me.*" [28] This is what Milton expressed vigorously in his harmonious verses.

> All these which in a moment thou behold'st,
> The kingdoms of the world to thee I give,
> For given to me I, give to whom I please,
> No trifle; yet with this reserve, not else,
> On this condition, if thou wilt fall down
> And worship me as thy Superior Lord;

---

[28] Tu ergo si adoraveris me haec tibi erunt omnia [SE: Tu ergo si adoraveris coram me erunt tua omnia - If thou therefore wilt worship me, all shall be thine.]. Gospel. Luke 4:7. Haec omnia tibi dabo si cadens adoraveris me [All these will I give thee, if falling down thou wilt adore me]. Gospel. Luke 4:7. [Luke 4:6].

Easily done, and hold them all of me;
For what can less so great a gift deserve?
   Milton's Paradise Regained. Book 4.

My purpose here is not to write the history of everything that can be told about Masonry. It is only to show the intrigues used by the Jesuits to bend the allegories and the initiations of the military order of the Templars to the four oaths of the indestructible *company*; to show their stubborn efforts to persuade that Free and Accepted Masonry is only the former order of the Templars. Then hopefully their initiates would delude into believing that the order of the Templars itself was only a jesuitic institution. And then what would they what would they make us believe about the mysteries of their order?

Although the name of their society originated from the name of Jesus Christ, born of yesterday, if one counts the centuries of nature, they would probably prove that they existed *before* Jesus Christ, before the Lamb without blemish, immolated, for the sins of the world. As his miraculous history is only attested by his Disciples, they cut it away from the Hebrew annals, and would make it adopt as an allegory; assertion that certainly would not be unlikely; because we would see them mentioning the Apocalypse, where is written that the *Lamb without blemish* has been immolated *since the creation of the world*[29]: they would then say that it would therefore not have been immolated to redeem the sins of the *created* world, since it had been *immolated* since the creation, and one would hear them exclaim victoriously like *Saint John:* If anyone has ears to hear, let him hear.[30]

From the name Saint John they made *Sanctus Joannes*, a jesuitic number. From this, they would prove very easily that the Revelation of Saint John points to the jesuitic society writing itself its own history. *Sanctus –S– Joannes –I–*. S.I. *Societas Jesuitarum!*

In Joseph, master Carpenter, they would find the grand *Carpenter* of the universe, the grand Architect of the world. Finally, what would I know about the likelihood they would find between the New and the Old Testaments. Saint Augustine states that the true meaning "of the *first three chapters* of the Genesis cannot be held without assigning to God things *unworthy of him,* and that it *is necessary to have resort to the allegory.*[31] They would tell as much about the New Testament; and the cross-examinations of the Templars, where it is proven that they only believed in one God and denied the Divinity of *Jesus Christ,* would only confirm their assertions to the eyes of these millions of initiates who feel quite honored of the pompous and resonant title of Templar.

---

[29] *In libro [vitae] agni qui occisus est ab origine mundi. Apocalypse* 13:8.

[30] *Si quis habet aurem audiat. Apocalypse* 13:9.

[31] *De Genesi contra Manichaeos* [SE: Saint Augustine. *On Genesis: A Refutation of the Manichees*. 401–415 C.E]. Book I.

1. Scottish Masonry and Templars

Yes, I admit, the beautiful actions and the courage of the knights of the Temple, who are certainly not without reproach, made their name harmonious in Europe, and it is well known that in all times it has been suspected that the former order of the Templars sometimes here and sometimes there, tried to reappear in Europe. But would a reasonable man dare accept *someone's word* that an *immediate* link exists between a society well respected today that counts among its members the first nobility of Europe, and an order persecuted in the fourteenth century by tortures and stakes!

However to judge soundly, I know that it is necessary to examine here with utmost caution an assertion that is not unlikely, and that so many millions of men in Europe *cherish* as *demonstrated*. The history of the fourteenth century attests that the Templars were closely united for the glory of an order that was dear to them and by a political goal and also by a secret very important for them. Now we cannot presume that the persecutions made against the order of the Templars could break all kinds of union between the isolated members. The bounds of recognition and friendship resist quite often the sword of despotism; an arbitrary sentence cannot change the nature of our leanings. While the tyrants could sometimes stop suddenly the course of opinions, this course has been observed to quickly flow like an unexpected torrent everywhere after awful devastations. Flame and sword will never extinguish an opinion: The danger to profess an opinion suffices to make someone dare to glorify it: The order of the Templars has indeed been thrown on the ground; however doesn't it seem that a certain *esprit de corps* always survive the sword of the executioners? Therefore, it would be rather natural to suspect that numerous Templars met in a house of solidarity, very generous towards persecuted unfortunates. There, glass in hand, they could have conceived hope to obtain by value the restoration of their order. One would even forgive that these warriors, covered with glorious injuries and feed in the horrors of the war, have sworn the death of their oppressors and the triumph of their order at the time of persecution. So the heart is forced to applaud the courageous Boadicea, leading her faithful Britons, who sworn revenge against *Suetonius* for the slaughters of her druids of Mona and exclaimed with them of a terrifying voice, while savoring the cup of the fraternity: "If it was Roman blood! Mona! Mona! Mona!"

Let's not decide anything: let's examine patiently what one holds for sacred in the *silence* of the *inner* sanctuary; let's lend to all an attentive and unbiased ear; if it is possible for us to contain our indignation! Let's be fair even with the wicked one: let's take for the oracle's voice, what the *intimate* priests reveal to us. Happy if we could recognize in it the honest and *beneficent* truth, the unique language of the one that deserves our respects! If on the contrary the consecrated underground from where exits the oracle's voice only exhales shouts of vengeance; oh my brothers! don't forget that *it is necessary to be man before being priest or soldier*! And again this other precept, this *first* precept engraved within your ancient columns: *There is nothing divine where there is nothing human!*

An oracle who softens only at the sight of the golden branch exclaimed: *God wants it*! And his priest arms you of a dagger! *To me, my brothers!* Let's throw down the bloody tripod, let's break the dagger of crime and may the infernal underground be closed forever!

Be frustrate, all ye stratagems of Hell,
And devilish machinations come to nought.[32]

The documents of which I am going to mention the main articles, that I translated on acts that I have been entrusted with *to make a public use of them*, continue, *say the ministers of the* Superior *Inconnus*, the explanation of the Masonic ceremonies, *reserved* to the Scottish masters, to initiate them in the *secret* and *inner* history of the society of the Masons!
This history was cleverly combined to appear genuine. However, in spite of the assertions of Mr. Smith, *instructed* Mason, and illustrious preacher of the Superior *Inconnus*, this *inner* history contradicts in all points what it written about the origin of the *enlightened* company. Let's have the Hierophant speak:

The secret of the Freemasons is explained by the history of the order of the Templars; famous [order] in the time of the Crusades of the European people. Their mysterious allegories represent the persecutions of Clement V and Philippe the Fair (le Bel); and the overthrow of the order, and the cruel death of the innocent Jacq. Burg. de Molay, Grand Master: it is again the history of the *secret institution* of some knights of the order escaped from the ruin, to keep its violated rights forever, and to hide its real shape under the shadows of a certain secret, until more favorable times that would permit it to tear the veil and to reappear publicly.
The name Mason was *adopted* because d'Aumont and seven Templars, disguised as Masons, fled into Scotland to escape the massacre, and because they worked there under the Mason's *profession* to not be recognized. The *profession* of Mason was found convenient to hide the persecuted order from all looks. The tools of the Masons provided for the *concepts* of the order favorable symbols that permitted to give it the outside appearance of a moral society, while serving for it as hieroglyphs to represent allegorically its entire history.
The Masons have to rebuild the Temple of Salomon. There is a moral meaning here but the true meaning is that one must *assist* the Templars in rebuilding their order. The compass, the mallet, the square, the line, etc. etc. mean prudence, ingenuity and the necessary precision for the Templars who had been dispersed, and

---

[32] Milton, J. *Paradise Regained.* 1671. Book One.

were as crushed under the remnants of their order, if they wanted to get ready for a triumph in the future.

By the name of Freemasons, one wanted to be distinguished from the working Masons and this word *Franc*, simultaneously English, French, and German, was *chosen* with intention. Besides its common meaning; it recalls again the fights in Palestine where the Templars were generally called *Francs* by the Oriental people, no matter their original nations. Still today the history of our Europe kept for the Templars the name *Francs*.

In addition, since the working Masons use signs to recognize themselves in their journeys, their symbols were used to veil the secret knowledge *possessed* by the knights Templars, and the most painful torments could not pull it out from them.

The order was named a *royal Order* and a *royal Art*, in memory of Baudouin, King of Jerusalem, who took the Templars under his protection; who lodged them in his palace, and helped them as king, to defend according to the major oath of the order, the widow, the orphan and the pilgrim.

It is called a Holly order because of the holy exercises and the holy rule, and the holy institutes that the Templars received from the popes and councils: from there come the names of *Worshipful*, *Most Worshipful*, and also the title of *brother*. The masters of the order are the *magistri* and the superiors. The lodge is the house of the Chapter, *compthuria domus*. The president is the master of the chair, *magister cathedrae*. The wardens are the procurators, *procuratores*. The other dignitaries of a lodge express allegorically the functions of the order and the place of official. The signs and tokens and the carpet, etc. are the symbols of the *insignia*, of the arms and *attires* of the order of the Templars. "

Pay close attention to the following paragraph and to the mysterious ideas and to the shape under which these ideas are presented.

"How is it that there is such an enormous difference in Masonry, taken in general, especially regarding ceremonies! etc. etc. Especially, why are some lodges perfect and well conducted in terms of goals and yet their constitution is far from the statutes of the Masonry?

In the history of the Masonry, the proof of the continuation of the order of the Templars under the name of Freemason is based on the continuation of d'Aumont, French knight and marshal of the order; on the other runaways who accompanied him in Scotland, and on the Grand Capitular or *compthour* Harris that they found there.

These people, one says,

This *hearsay* is rather pleasing in the secret history of the inner sanctuary.

"These people, one says, *invented* Frank-masonry; and they *hid* within it the order of the Templars: but *in such a way* that the order of Templars or *the true secret* of Freemasons always had to be successively the property of their children, although Masonry accepted people of all state, all nations, and all Christian religions.

Here is the state of things, always the same, for more than two hundred fifty years: however the history of Masonry says nothing if the order withdrew exclusively within Scotland and England, or if it spread its mysteries among other peoples of the continent; although it kept for us a chronological table of the name of the main Superiors and Grand Masters of the order, among which one finds some Scottish, English, French and German people.

No matter what, it *results* from these facts about our Masonic history that the order of the Masons either comes straight down from the ancient upholders of the order of the Templars, or that their descendants created our constitutions.

Now if our Masonic history states than only the Scottish Masters, after one hundred and fifty years, transferred *to others* their hereditary right to the order of the Templars, to give to themselves more strength and more reach; if the history of our Europe shows only that since approximately one hundred years, the *first traces* of Freemasonry in the islands of Great Britain; and if ourselves, everywhere we stop our looks on the globe, we see in general in the immense number of our lodges, the best order, a good police, wise laws and the noblest and most ancient simplicity, we are forced to believe that it is to the primitive instruction and the original construction that took place in Great Britain, that Freemasonry owes the *concordance* and the *unity* of its regulations; and the authority of its lodges and its Chapters.

The master of the lodge behind *his table* and the wardens facing him, and the brothers on the sides represent entirely the ancient capitular sessions of the ecclesiastical brothers; fratrum ecclesiasticorum; and their chapters; the master seats in the Orient because the Grand Masters of the order of the Templars, in its splendor, had a county seat or general domicile in the oriental countries, and that it is in Orient that the order of the Templars began to bloom and succeed. The sub-commanders lived in the western countries (that is Europe) and it was in Europe that the complete ruin of the order was prepared.

Masonry accepts indifferently men of all religions, because the Templars admitted without distinction in their order members of the Greek Church or the Latin Church.

The manner to propose a candidate in the order of the Freemasons is precisely the one used in the former order. The black and white

1. Scottish Masonry and Templars

> balls ballot determined the reception of the Novice in the ancient order like in ours.
> The son of a Freemason can obtain dispensations of age to be received in the order."

It is sufficient for him to be 18 years old: when a novice is not the son of a Freemason, he must be twenty-five years old, according to the rule and the strict observance, that is, he must have the necessary age for priesthood.

> "A dispensation of age is granted to the *male child* of a Mason to show that the order of the Templars, believed shattered, is perpetuated by the children of the knights who escaped the persecution of the fourteenth century and that these children are considered at birth as the members and the keepers of the order of the Templars in their families.
> The dark room and the frights of the reception signify that the Templars, upon entering into the order, don't foresee that their fidelity to maintain its glory would expose them to the exile, to the tortures, and to infamous torments.
> The disarmament, the stripping of the clothes, the left breast and the right knee uncovered, means that it is necessary to strip one's former clothes to *take the religious attire* of the order: these emblems also express the misery and the indigence of the Templars who were either fleeting or tortured cruelly. You are being stripped from all metals, because the wealth of the Templars brought forth the desire and the *cupidity* of the *powerful ones*, and caused the ruin of the order.
> Once again, this signifies the oath of poverty, *votum paupertatis*, and the poverty of the *first* Templars.
> What is the meaning of the blindfold and the sword on the heart during the travels?

This ceremony is abandoned in France and in England, or at least is not practiced everywhere today. In the *observantia lata*, or late observance, in Germany; in Russia and in Sweden it is upheld with rigor.

> "To be blindfolded and having the sword on the heart represents the unfortunate Templars; the *victims* of the persecution who would be led to tortures by the executioners, or would be stricken by a sword without ceremony.
> The candidate's examination is the emblem of the judicial cross-examinations of the Templars.
> One introduces you in lodge *while the aprons rustle* [au bruit des tabliers]."

Ceremony essentially observed in some English lodges and abandoned or rarely used in France.

> "And in spite of the accuracy of his answers, the novice is, so to speak, *rejected* in the room. This noise and this length of time are the emblems of the tumult and inhumanity that accompany the cross-examinations of the Templars dragged from court to court to pull the *wanted confession* from them, before spilling their blood. "
>
> One walks you three times around the carpet. What *happens there* is the emblem of the news unforeseen of the persecutions against all superiors of the order of the Templars and the deadly stroke against the order.
>
> The Candidate placed before the master is interrogated brutally; his trust is tested, etc. etc. etc. It is again the emblem of the ferocious manner with which the judges conducted the cross-examinations of the Templars and offered them to choose liberty or an infamous death, to incite them to betray the order and to reveal its mysteries. The Templars, always faithful, didn't reveal anything.
>
> The oath of the Freemasons represents the former vows of the recipient in the order of the Templars; it was also by an oath that all Templars committed to hide the mysteries *brought* to their order.
>
> After the oath the candidate is brought back on the doorstep of the Temple, and this step is accompanied by a large number of ceremonies. It is the emblem of the perils to which the brother is exposed by his engagements towards the order of the Templars, by which he *acquired* persecution, banishment and death.
>
> One removes to the candidate his blindfold: he is stricken by a beam of light that dies suddenly: simultaneously one shouts to his ear: *Sic transit gloria mundi*! So passes the glory of the world. Then he sees all swords of the brothers turned against his heart. It is the emblem of the extinction of the outside splendor of the order of the Templars, and of all swords of death altered by the blood of its faithful knights: it is again these same persecutions that are represented to us by the *exchange of blood* at the reception of the novice in the order of the Freemasons."

This exchange of blood is symbolically in use in all lodges of the former Swedish observance. Today in *France* it appears to me that the symbol of the bleeding has been substituted by an interpretation that is very clear for those who know the hidden goal of the Superior Inconnus; but that is far from reminding an exchange of blood between two brothers: the new ceremony always announces the spilling of foreign blood. As for the ceremony of *blood exchange*, I don't dare to say. However, it seems to me that it clearly suggests a last degree of brotherly link. By a sublime devotion to *friendship* and *truth*, it might have taken place sometimes, very seriously, as to attach *one's heart to one's friend's heart*. In such way both people would *reveal* to one another, by turns and by a feeling *that became shared by both of them,* the disorders of fear, the enthusiasm of hope, or at least the perpetual certainty of one another's existence!

"The number three double three, triple three, is explained by the history of the order of the Templars: the three degrees of Masonry represent the three phases of growth of the order: it is the emblem of the triple generalate; the number three at the novice's reception and everything that occurs then by three at the admission of the first degree has relationship only to the generalate.

In the second phase of the order of the Templars there were six generals or six leaders: this explains the number six of the Fellowcraft degree in Masonry."

In its highest splendor the order of the Templars had nine or three times three generals. This number was given to the degree of Master Mason: the number nine was not dedicated without reason in the order of the Templars. Nine knights first met as founders of the order; and then they separated by three until King Baudouin granted them for home the *House* of the Temple. Three times nine knights, or twenty-seven knights, kept the order until the year 1127, when they deputized nine knights to the council of Troyes to obtain the rule of the order and the confirmation of the order and the rule.

Then the twenty-seven knights divided into three quarters and chose Jerusalem, Aleppo, and Caesarea. Every quarter was composed of three times nine knights. Soon each company of nine knights elected a Superior, *Superior,* and the nine Superiors a Prefect, *Proefectum.* This explains the mysterious gradation from number three to number nine *that shines eminently* in the Company of the nine generals.

The member elect in Masonry *receives* a white apron, etc. etc. It is the emblem of the *investiture* of the Templars: the white apron and the white gloves represent the *garments of the order* granted by the pope and the Council of Troyes; and the trowel is the *cross of the order* that must remain hidden.

The military and dispersed Templars had their signs and their *passwords* to recognize themselves in time and place. This gave the idea to provide some to the Freemasons as well. The sign of the collar and the hand on the heart, and the various signs of the degrees of Apprentice, Fellowcraft and Master, relate to the *oral tradition* of the revenge drown by the unselfish remaining Templars against those betrayed them.

The words *Jackin, Boaz* and *Mac-Benacs* deserve a particular attention. They eternalize, without one suspecting it, in the order of the Freemasons, the name of the unfortunate Grand Master of the ancient order of the Templars. The three initial letters give J. B. M. or, according to the Masonic number, *Jacq. Burg. Molay,* whose particular history is kept allegorically in the Degree of Master under the name of the Grand Master Hiram, massacred by the fellows at the time of Salomon.

The title of brother granted to the candidate after his reception, and the kiss that the *master*, who is at the head of the company, gives to him while sending him back in the society of the *brethren*, are the emblem of the fraternity, and of the fraternal kiss in use in the former order: *Osculum fraternitatis*.

The Grand Master Hiram, murder by his rebellious fellows, could very well be" ---

Could very well be! *Hearsay* and *maybes*! Such a certainty in the secret history of the Inner Sanctuary!

"Could very well be in our history the sub-prior of Montfaucon, *Carolus de Monte Carmel*, Charles of Mount Carmel; whose murder was the first attack carried against the order by traitors. The three strokes given at the reception of the mastery, *would then be* truly historic; as well as the *acacia* or thorn bush used by the murderers to hide the place where they had buried the body of the sub-prior. These same symbols also have *enough relationship* with the knights of the sub-prior; not seeing the sub-prior around them. They start searching for his body and found it under a stack of thorn branches which raised their suspicions. The cadaver was exhumed, and then buried in the temple, as it is said during the reception of master. Since then, it is *symbolized* by all the trials he must undergo. But one could further take these emblems, *under another point of view*, as the death of the Grand Master Molay; the new lights, around the *murdered master*." ---

The recipient now called *master*, to make believe that his reception is the exact allegory of the Grand Master Molay cannot strictly be called *master*. At the time of a first ceremony of his reception to the mastery, the recipient is still strictly only a Fellowcraft mason, intended to the degree of Master mason which he might not be granted; either because he suddenly dies from fright, or because some other major and unforeseen misfortune occurs at the time of the initiation and disperses at once all the brothers.

"The nine lights around the murdered master represent evidently the Grand Master of the nine generals of the order of the Templars: the *sacramental word* and the answer of the wardens: *The flesh leaves the bones*, are applicable only to the *dry* and burnt remains of the Grand Master.

The three travels that the brother Mason as a Master makes from orient to occident, from occident to south, from south to occident, *under the inscription* of *memento mori* or *think about death*,

represent the journeys of the Grand Master Molay. He left the *county seat* of the Grand Generalate established in the island of Cyprus, arrived in Paris, then left Paris for the Court of Rome for his defense, and then he was sent back by the pope to Paris, for his judgment to be pronounced there. The three strikes that the master receives during his reception from the brothers armed with paper rollers, represent allegorically the accusations, the judgment and the death of the Grand Master. The traitors and the murderers are Noffodei, Pope Clement V and the King of France Philippe the Fair (le Bel). *Our history* says that after the stake burnt out, around noon, the body of the Grand Master was buried under the debris of a building; but that the Templars came at midnight to remove secretly the body of their Grand Master, and buried it close to a mountain. For this reason, a lodge is presumed to always open up *at full noon*. Our history says that the Templars planted a thorn on the tomb of the Grand Master. This thorn, a sign used in tribute to the Templars, served the Scottish Masters who, taking advantage of King Edward's incursions in France, exhumed the bones of Molay which were then buried secretly in front of the high altar of the Église du temple [Templar Church] in Paris. *It is said* that *within a year* God himself avenged the death of the Grand Master against the two assassins, Clement V and Philippe the Fair (le Bel).[33]
However the real intention cannot be determined here."

There is here a curiously authentic history, *obvious and secret*, and kept *with religious care* in the inner sanctuary. In the last degree it is read quickly and by grace to the Scottish Master.

Let's seize the beneficial thread; let's hurry and escape from the maze we are locked in. Fanaticism is here, I recognized it from its blindfold and from its dagger that gropes for a victim: ambition applauds him and caresses him with one hand while it binds him with the other, without him whispering, or [binds] him in a way that he cannot escape, regardless of what he does.

Irons are always irons. Some brethren say that the Masonic chains are children's games, invented to amuse one instant people *without malice*. As for me, I know that at the first signals all slaves are chained one to the others. Does one play with a dagger? Game or not, it is a vile weapon, that is not made for the hand of a French!

Could there that soon this God of the French people will reign all over Europe? This God who only wants famous martyrs and a generous, human, and honorable devotion. This God who is finally ready to strike down forever the god of the *monks*, the god of vengeances, that only demands victims, that only creates executioners. May honor, that is to say humanity without which there is no honor, be forever sacred to the French people!

---

[33] [SE: Philip and Clement V both died within a year of Molay's execution, Clement succumbing to a long illness and Philip in a hunting accident.]

Honor speaks, it is sufficient; these are our oracles."[34]

Vile fanaticism, I loathe you; I would like to be able to despise you, I would not hate you!
May French people remember how easy they acted while seduced during the Crusades: the first occurred on foreign lands: but France, instead of freeing itself, ran to the weapons; and here again, in the eighteenth century, what an enormous difference!

> "Tis no idle crowd raising a tumult,
> but the fatal zeal of the whole blinded people,[35]
> And hell covering all with its gloomy vapors,"
> Can change LIGHT in impure darkness.[36]

> O thievish Night,
> Why shouldst thou, but for some felonious end,
> In thy dark lantern thus close up the *stars*
> That Nature hung in *heaven*, and filled their lamps
> With everlasting oil to give due light
> To the misled and lonely *traveller?*[37]

Let's resume the tenacious story of the inner sanctuary where after having assured us that such allegories were *evidently* the emblem of such or such fact, one nearly adds immediately:

> "that the primary intention and the real meaning of the masonic ceremonies cannot be determined with certainty.
> "*It is sufficient to know*," say the Superior Inconnus, "that the Grand Master *Hiram* is a person whose murder led to the ruin of the order of the Templars; that the death of the *sub-prior* began the persecutions, and that the torment of Molay led to the disgrace of the order. But the real hieroglyph of the name *Hiram* is explained by all its letters; they express in summery the fate of the Templars: Hugo H – Initiatus I – Ignes I – Raptus R – Atrocissimo A – Molay M. Altogether, this gives, H I I R A M."

---

[34] [SE: Racine, Jean. Iphigénie en Aulide (Iphigenia in Aulis).]
[35] [SE: Racine, Jean. *Iphigénie*. Scene 3. The original is "Eurybate: Tis no idle crowd Raising a tumult, but the fatal zeal Of the whole camp."]
[36] [SE: Racine, Jean. *Esther*. Prologue. Piety. The original is "Hell, covering all with its gloomy vapors, has cast shadows on even the holiest eyes."]
[37] See Milton's *Comus*: a Mask.

1. Scottish Masonry and Templars

Isn't this abridged history of the fate of the Templars of the last ridicule! That the Jesuits thought that one would not be going to deepen their Greek etymologies because of the small number of learned people that probe the roots of this language, is a rather natural thing; but would they dare imagine that there would not be a Mason who would say at the sight of a rhapsody of Latin words: This is not an obscure meaning, it is clearly an absurdity. Their history offers no correct meaning in Latin, no links, no coherence. *Hugo Initiatus, igne raptus atrocissimo Molay,* "Hugo initiated, Molay consumed by the most atrocious fire."

The meaning that one could find in the French translation would be clear enough: The day Hugo was initiated, Molay was thrown in the flames: but Latin doesn't permit this interpretation, because then it would have been necessary to write: *Hugone initiato*; which would not have changed anything however to the initial letters: but does one think about everything, even when one is Jesuit? Would there be rather another mental meaning in the Inner sanctuary? We didn't totally forget Pascal in France, and we know the resource of the possible opinions of these worthy and virtuous Fathers! – Fathers! What sacred word they haven't searched!

Add to the gibberish of their *abridged* history, that they altered the name of Hiram, dedicated verb. This word is always written with five letters, they write it here with six letters, HIIRAM.

> "In the lodges, while pulling, sometimes to the right, sometimes to the left, the Master *word Mac-Benac,* one gave him numerous interpretations."

It is again a small confession of *their good faith* and I acknowledge this. To not say everything, this is to be cautious: one must not say everything. But to *lie!* to lie to *one's brother!* The lie, because it is vile by nature, always leads to crime.

> "This word of *Mac-Benac,* so differently interpreted in the lodges, is nothing more than a word by *convention,* under which the successor of Molay at the generalate of the order of the Templars, secretly perpetuated, hid its continuation in Scotland.
> The blue color attached to the degree of master is the color adopted by the secret order of the Templars. *This is why* one is armed in lodge in the three degrees of Freemasonry. The naked sword at the opening of the lodge indicates the military order and the knighthood of the former Templars.
> Besides, it was *prudent, wise* and *necessary,* and it is still today very important that the Freemasons *play* the ceremonies, without knowing anything about their real meaning."

Poor Masons! Look at how you are treated! Don't you see what is revealed to you every day about effrontery and cupidity? Expectations, and daggers, and homage, isn't this therefore not a rather expressive language? You don't hear what your Superior Inconnus tell you bluntly: Our secret history, communicated to the perfect masters in the inner sanctuary, can never be a secret *history*, since it is printed in detail in the mysterious works of our *instructed* Masons. Therefore each of you imitate the instructed Masons in your own manner. For the honor of Masonry, we need audacious people who will tremble under our eyes; we will load them with *irons* and call these *ribbons, crosses, embassies* or *principalities*. People will first laugh at this; but little-by-little we will become richer and more powerful: some ambitious one will need our money or our weapons, and it will be our turn to laugh. This is already the *shadow* of a religion, and this is a first success: our devoted apostles are already in bigger numbers than those of the Son of Mary. You know what they were some centuries ago, and what their descendants are today: see, by their fast success, what can be made one day with caution and patience. Boast our mysteries; whispering it to ones' ear, it is safer. Speak with pump of our Temples, of our sublime works, of our ancient secrets; and if we don't have any; we must have some, that is to say, to pretend to have some; this is the masterpiece of a grand style of politics. Do you want to write? Let the Mason elevated at the last degree speaks *at ease* of the ceremonies: but that what he doesn't say is always the sacred! The A and H Masonry, or Adon-Hiramite Masonry, dedicated, not without motive, to the *instructed* Masons, hides carefully the passwords like a big mystery, although they are printed and sold publicly in England and elsewhere. And yet it doesn't matter; they cannot be blamed; they always spoke skillfully to bring some victims to the priests of the holy Temple. The multitude easily gives its respect, its heart and its money *for words*; it will pay *for words* without whisper; and for everything deemed useful in our intentions to delude it.

You, in particular, our very worthy brothers; elected and Scottish masters, don't fear to reveal openly our most secret mysteries: because, without having here to resort to our famous maxims on mental restrictions, it is good to remove from you all scruple to end our *secret* history, so much boasted in public, by these solemn words of the favorite illustrious ones of our grand Priest, always behind the curtain:

> "If one revealed our entire *secret* history given at the highest degree
> of Masonry, NOTHING would be betrayed: one would only have the
> impenetrable envelope of our mysteries."

Specifically, let us not lose sight of this essential article of the acts of Scottish Masonry; a little patience, and one will know how to seize the simple truth under the mystical jumble of the Superior Inconnus.

After having finished the solemn reading of the secret history of the inner sanctuary, the brother devoted to research has become extremely attentive by some strange declamations on the mysteries of the Templars and on the persecutions and on the continuation of the order have made him extremely

1. Scottish Masonry and Templars

attentive. However, instead of instructing him, one is wisely content with sending him back with *theses* and problems that put him exactly back where he had left.

However for the honor of the order he is carefully encouraged to really meditate on these illusory and problematic *questionings*; he is invited to increase them by particular research on the old and modern history: and he is advised to carry all without indiscretion, one makes him hope that some good superiors, some conservative fathers of the mysterious knowledge, will certainly reveal to him after some years of trials, what he could never get without their help, worthy of homage from the entire admiring nature.

We are going to place here the theses and problems of the unknown superiors, so that the thinking being can evaluate by himself the real goal of the Jesuitical society.

1. "The *Scottish master* is undoubtedly the Templar who perpetuated, in secret, in his family, the unlucky order of the persecuted Templars.
2. He needed a veil, because he wanted to return to the families of the other nations their hereditary right to the order of the Templars.
3. One found the veil in the symbols of the overturned order, and one started to woven the history of the mysteries of the order, the secret circumstances of its misfortunes, its conservation and its propagation.
4. Like the Freemasons who *symbolized* by their Jackin, Boaz, and Mac-Benac, J. B. M. *Jac. Burg. Molay*, their grand master, the Scottish masters dedicated the memory of their benefactor *Aumont*, keeper and restorer of the order of the Templars, in their word *Notuma*, which is the anagram of his name.
5. For the Masons brethren, the *three*, *six* and *nine* lights are the emblem of the *three*, *six* and *nine* successively established Generals, and also of the nine founders of the order. The Scottish masters represent by the four lights the four major chapters [capitulary], *compthores*, who perpetuated the order in the Scottish Island of Mull [Mals].
6. Again following the Freemasons who created their *signs* and their *strokes* according to their number *three* that they have called *triangle*, the Scottish adjusted their *signs* and their *steps*, etc. according to their number four that they call a *square*.
7. The Scottish [degree] rope is received on the collar to symbolize the destiny of Noffodei who was strangled in a secret chapter in *Montfaucon*.
8. The recipient, *adorned* with this reward of the treason, receives grace *as a result of his knowledge*, he is taught that the master *still lives, is standing up and asks for his help*.
9. But for what kind of science is Scottish master granted forgiveness?
10. Did the former Scottish masters, and therefore the Templars, possess some hidden secrets?

11. By any chance, did anyone have in mind this mysterious knowledge when the apprentice was given the name of *Tubalcain*?
12. Under the number of their three Masonic columns STRENGTH, WISDOM and BEAUTY, *Fortitudo, Sapientia* and *Pulchritudo*; F.S.P. might there be a hidden number *three* which would be *the whole art* of the Scottish?

These three initial letters F.S.P. are *the whole art of the Scottish.* Could they not clearly mean, according to the jesuitic number *fraternitas societatis patrum*, "fraternity of the society of the fathers"?

19. The immense wealth necessary to the construction of Salomon's temple was immense and the wealth of the former Templars was inconceivable. Could these possessions have a same source?
20. Powerful men persecuted and dismembered the order; slaughtered, delivered for torture and tortured the brothers of the order. Could it be that their goal was to discover the hidden sources of so much wealth?"
21. The unknown source of these treasures; could it be the *lost* that one looks for in the perpetuated order? Could it be to find it, that the catechism of the Scottish masters sends them travelling by the whole earth.
22. Is the order already very advanced in its intentions?
23. How can we serve the views of the order? "

Further details on the history of the inner sanctuary, deemed appropriate to be called secret by some, would become rather useless. One thousand beams of light had to pierce the darkness made to envelop the mysterious tripod; and the inner sanctuary is enlightened enough, it seems to me, for the attentive eye that likes to analyze independently. What I believe to have proven here, by the excerpts of the acts of the highest degree of the free and accepted Masonry, is the *belief* in an *immediate* link between the Society of the Freemasons and the former order of the Templars. This is not all that can be discovered about the intentions of the superiors of the order there: one recognizes their *main goal* there: their intention to *persuade* the initiates that the Mysteries of their order contain an inexhaustible *gold mine*, with the promise that this will be only pure gold one day. And if we consider the universal tendency of average people towards wealth; and their thirst of gold, even it involves blood, human blood, we must admit that the matters of the Superior Inconnus are a true master piece of infernal mischief.
Is there anything more absurd than to believe the Templars of being gold makers? The confidant of the genius and the customs of their centuries, the famous historian David Hume will probably not be looking for the origin of their wealth in such sources: but what can we do? One addresses ignorant people, thoughtless people, and further, men accustomed to believe; and besides people believe what their heart wants so comfortably!

1. Scottish Masonry and Templars

It was at the cost of their blood and their might, that the Templars acquired their vast possessions in the Holly Land; besides the favorable circumstances of the crusades that contributed to enrich all kind of adventurers, they found again in their greed, in their insolence, in their pride and in their fearlessness, the means always efficient to increase their wealth.
If they had had the secret to make gold, the Templars would be only more despicable for having so many time violated their knight's word, committed for a little bit of money; for having committed so many cruelties, in order to gain some of it. No matter the price, they were in need. Possessing the secret to make gold, could they have given so many opportunities to be hated because of their rapines and their baseness? Let's remember only the complaints of the Patriarch of Jerusalem, whom they refused to pay for the tithe; and the thirteen hundred Byzantine coins and other goods that they refused to the Bishop of Tiberias. Let's remembers coldly therefore their conduct towards King Leo of Armenia, and the possessions that they had in his kingdom, valued to twenty one thousand Byzantine coins, and again the rights usurped from King Henri III of England; and all these robberies that history blames them openly. Then the magical *crucible* vanishes unless we want to believe the Templars much more guilty than they are, because to the eyes of all men unbiased and without prejudice who study their history, they are guilty: and the atrocious complaints filled against them by the secular princes, the ecclesiastical princes, and especially the popes were not ungrounded.
Not that I want here to reproach them; as one did, that they were required by oath to increase the goods of the order by all possible means, just or unjust; that finally all was allowed and legitimate to them, up to violating one's faith, to enrich the order. These assertions are not legally proved. As for the other facts that I have just put forward they are known universally and are sufficient to convince us that the secret to make gold was not the unknown source of the big wealth of the Templars.
I have no intention to tarnish the glory of the Templars: an unlucky father will accuse his son of being mad to save him of an infamous torment. The historian must tell the facts; he is not asked what he thinks or what he wants but what he saw. It is the testimony and not the opinion of the historian that matters to me, said Bacon. If I spoke of the usurpations and the robberies of a crowd of Templars, it because it is appropriate and useful to communicate this truth, proved by all our histories, to thousand of honest Masons. They all have something else to do than to gather and to compare general histories in hundred volumes: an abyss, a chaos, a sea without shores!
We are far from trying to remove from the alleged descendants of the Templars the high ideas that they conceived of the famous exploits and their *alleged* ancestors. On the contrary we believe to have found among them some laudable things that are to them as much more honor than one would not have suspected them, in a society of rural and wild warriors, in times of fanaticism. As our profession here is the analysis, it is up to the philosopher reader to climb by himself on the desolate ruins that we indicate to him.

Collected on the remnants of a former world, he will see his thought filling an immense interval, and enlarge and spread with a horizon that will have no more boundaries for him. And then it is up to him to judge if the Superiors of the present Society of Freemasons would not have found in the order of the Templars something else more reasonable than the sublime *materials* that they give *to work on* to their favorites within the Inner Sanctuary.

Everything that we brought back from real sources of the wealth of the former Templars leaves no hope to the good Freemasons to ever learn from their superior, as descendants of the Templars, the *secret* to make gold. Therefore, the link between Masonry and the order of the Templars, on that point of view at least, is nothing more than a chimera that one could easily abandon to the madman. A daily experience can prove to be painful in that it can turn the reason of the wisest: I knew in my visits in lodge, a good family father who worked fourteen to fifteen years to extract all French catechisms, all signs of our French degrees, and who is certain that the measures of the tomb of Adon-Hiram are of the highest antiquity, and that they represent the necessary weights and measures to make gold. His immense research, useless to their author, were not so for me. They help me in verifying the jesuitic number on precious acts of Free and Accepted Masonry: what is rather strange in the result of the research of my untiring Freemason, is that he sees in priests only ignorant masons, who play like most of ours with *ceremonies that they don't understand*: then he does not know what to think anymore, it is an abyss, he gets lost in it; he sees in the mysteries of Masonry only the mysteries of Christianity. As he knows neither Latin nor Greek, nor any foreign language, the eternal quotes that he suspects false or frivolous often stop him in his work: I suggested to him the *Antiquité dévoilée* and the *Christianisme dévoilé* by Boulanger;[38] since then it is impossible to answer to him: today's Masons are only priests, and the body of our clergy is only an illegitimate branch, rejected from the august mysteries of the *Adonhiramite* Masonry, "entrusted into Adam by God himself and coming to us *without alterations* by Adam from Methuselah to Noah."[39]

If the immediate link between the Adonhiramite Masonry and the order of the Templars is obviously only an audacious lie as for the secret to make gold,

---

[38] [SE: Both works have since been attributed to H.T. D'Holbach. *Antiquité dévoilée par ses usages {Antiquity Unveiled through its Customs}*, 1766, is not to be confused with *Antiquity Unveiled* by J.M. Roberts, 1892, *Christianisme dévoilé*, 1761, has been translated as *Christianity Unveiled* by W.M. Johnson, 1795 and as *Christianity Unveiled by Baron d'Holbach – A Controversy in Documents (Rescued from Obscurity)* by D.M. Holohan, 2008.]

[39] Dr Dodd in [George] Smith's Work. As I am printing these Essays, a very curious work has just been produced in England, whose purpose is to prove that today's priests are absolutely only a sect *rejected from within the ancient Masonry*. [See *The Use and Abuse of Freemasonry*].

1. Scottish Masonry and Templars

let's look further. Let's see if it there could be some likely opinion to support an assertion that tickles the heart of our Freemasons!

To solve the doubts of a reader who only want to know the truth, I am going to try to compare everything that has been published about the present institutions of the Society of the Freemasons in Europe, with the institutions of the former order of the Templars. How happy I would be if I can untangle the real secrets of the Templar brothers: because then, without pulling the veil of the Inner Sanctuary away , all Mason initiated into the major mysteries will be able to decide for himself if the ceremonies of the former order were kept. Furthermore, *being more familiar with the Templars*, he will know how to judge without our help how much he can trust the unknown superiors who promise the worthy Scottish masters a part of the precious repository of the mysteries of the Templars.

What can be know today of the inner ceremonies and of the institution of the former order of the Templars is consigned in the voluntary depositions made by the knights of the order in Britain, where they were free. The authenticity of these testimonies cannot be contested. The judicial information from Clement V, in alliance with King Philippe, could rather be suspected inaccurate, as accommodating confessions pulled in the anguish of the torture, or by the hope to get a wanted forgiveness. Now, after having examined if the confessions of the Templars interrogated and executed in France agreed with the other depositions of the free knights, in England, in Ireland, and In Scotland, we thought that wherever these *two revelations* were compliant, there were for us a truth to collect.

We compared the free depositions and the confessions of the Templars in the scholar works of the German authors: they are the only ones who wrote accurately about this famous time of the history of our modern Europe.[40]

Brilliant critiques have demonstrated with evidence that among the Templars there were three professions.

The first reception in the order of the Templars was public and in conformity with the public rule of the order known by all novices: in the examinations,

---

[40] See the essay of Nicolaï on the order of the Templars and the Society of the Freemasons, *Versuch über den Tempelherr Orden*, etc. [Christoph Friedrich Nicolaï, *Versuch über die Besschuldigungen welch dem Tempelherrnorden gemacht worden und über dessen Geheimniss; nebst einem Anhange uber das Entstehen der Freimaurergesellschaft {An Essay on the accusations made against the Order of Knights Templar and their mystery; with an Appendix on the origin of the Fraternity of Freemasons}*, 1782] and the history of the Templars by the Dr. Anton, *Geschicte of the Tempelhern*, etc. [Dr. Carl Gottlob Von Anton , Versuch einer Geschichte des Tempelherren ordens {*An Essay on the Order of Knights Templar*}, 1779, translated in French as *Essai sur l'histoire de l'Ordre des Templiers*, 1840, by E. Fraissient and *Untersuchung uber das Gehemniss und die Gebrauche der Tempelherren {An Inquiry into the Mystery and Usages of the Knights Templar }*, 1782.].

this reception is called *the authorized and the good profession*. Nothing but honest things happened then, and it is not surprising that so many brave Templars, who probably only knew the first profession, held with confidence that all reproaches made against the order were false and slanderous.

Through the second profession, one became more closely united to the knights: it was necessary there to disown the *Divinity* of the Son of Mary, to trample underfoot on *his cross* and to swear to never abandon the order: this last oath, given the ceremony of the profession, was indispensable; no one understands its necessity immediately. As a mark of their admission to the *secret* knighthood, they were given a belt of linen and forced to carry it secretly at all times under their clothes. This reception in the examinations is named the second profession *against faith*. According to the confessions of a few Templars, it appears that the novice kissed the President who greeted him in an indecent manner; in the manner of the popes as some authors say, but according to them, they kissed their professed authority on "parts not intended for this use." However some good knights admitted to the second profession denied *this ceremony*, and we must assume that the master of the assembly could freely exempt from the kiss of peace all man of honor who didn't need such a test to keep faithfully a secret whose revelation could bring on the order of the Templars persecutions, death; and even more cruel for warriors, infamy!

Then maybe the soft kiss was only given during to the third reception?

During the third and last profession, they were received in the number of the elected ones who *governed* the order and constituted the general chapter of the voters to the grand mastery. In this general chapter, they were granted the view of *one symbolic* image as the *grand secret of the order.*

Besides the belt of linen of the *secret* knighthood, or of the second profession, the Templars received another belt to hide under their clothes. This other belt was given either according to the rule of a sacred order, or to express a chastity vow or maybe rather like a distinct mark of the knighthood. As for the hearsay that the belt of linen was given to the Templars only for *magical* purposes, they have not yet been confirmed in any publications of the criminal procedures of the Templars.

In general, these are the main ceremonies of the three professions of the order of the Templars. I let the Main Scottish masters reconcile their higher degree with such an institution. As for me, I don't find a shadow of direct resemblance. However, I will avoid stating that it is impossible that the Masonic ceremonies have not been based on the Templar ceremonies, by a clever politics that used ingeniously for its intentions some symbols while ignoring their true meaning; or that it cared little that they arrived to the posterity without alteration: all institution feel the hand of the time. Regardless of what Mr. Smith says, I am far from believing that this mysterious knowledge, reserved to its worthy initiates, arrived unaltered by thousands of successors, from Adam's hands to the Superior Inconnus.

Oh TIME, oh time, some men claiming to be public teachers seem to ignore your power! It is your flow that ceaselessly kneads different faces for fleeting stages. It is you that devoured innumerable nations in a wink of a bird and rejected from your breast a *new world*. Again and again, you have kneaded our globe entirely!

Poor little globe, is it necessary therefore to have so many sublime and ancient revelations to know you? You who, humanly talking, only contain *matter*, always the same; and *sounds*, and *shapes*, that are always the blueprint, the reunion, the mirror and the reflection of a bigger number of shapes, that necessarily *improve* under the *perpetual movement* of Nature, by the influence of *mind* and Matter!

Let's stop our looks on the major secret confided to the Templars in the third and last profession. Could we bring some clarity on this obscure allegory so respected by the former order? And even more surprising, could this be therefore this famous *hereditary treasure* that the Superior Inconnus reserve for their faithful *servants*?

Let us open randomly the history of our Europe in these days of anarchy, when the famous Hugh Capet had the singular honor to establish THE ETERNAL FAMILY on the throne of the French people;[41] let us refer to the bloody centuries when so many popes, like Urban, Gregory, Pascal, Alexander or Adrian, armed with *invisible swords* deposed the sovereigns. This is when we see in the history of the scheming of the popes, the marvelous influence of the *auricular* confession on the events of our Europe. It was especially essential for the sovereign pontiff and for the *representatives* of God that this institution so useful to their politics was declared holy and necessary to enter in the Heavens that would be open and closed according to their whims. The Templars, most of whom laymen, were not the most hurried people to bite into the pontifical fishhook. Far from biting into it, they persuaded one another that they could absolve themselves mutually from their sins and as efficiently as the pope and all his priests. Therefore they confessed one other. Additionally, they believed that the Grand Master could even absolve them from non confessed sins and even from the *divine influences* of THE EXCOMMUNICATION. At the time, this sentence of *damnation* was so frightening that in the depth of their palace and their restful kingdom, audacious but religious kings would be shattered.

An institution where the absolution from the papal damnation occurred behind closed doors; where the *thunderbolts* of the Holly Father were ridiculed. Considering that this occurred at a time of superstition and ignorance, I dare say that this society resembled in no ways the assemblies of our Scottish masters. There was there at least an important secret for all brethren; a secret that would still be one in our beautiful and so enlightened days; a secret known by all initiated brothers; it was an awful secret in the

---

[41] For about nine hundred years, the Bourbon family sits on the throne, without interruption, unique example among Kings. [SE: "Eternal family" is a term unique to Bonneville, also used in his work *Histoire de l'Europe Moderne* and rather astute: overall, dozens of branches of the Capetian dynasty still exist throughout Europe.]

fourteenth century. In a way, could Clement V, then pope and king of kings, be excused for having persecuted the order of the Templars so intensely?

The proof that the ceremony of the second or third profession by which the novice disowned Christ and trampled his cross underfoot was a secret interesting all superior brothers: often the recipient was forced, sword at hand, to resolve to this abnegation. If the strangeness of the proposition astonished him until fanaticism, he would be locked up until he became more compliant. The heads of the order had too much interest to hide their secret to leave anyone who could betray them go carelessly.

It is said that the biggest secret of the order was this mysterious image exposed with solemnity in the general chapter. In the examinations of the Templars, one calls this image *idolum*, *caput*, idol, head, idol *in the image of a man*, bearded idol made *in figuram Baffometi*, *in the image of Baffomet*, idol, on which was painted *the image of Baffomet*, *ubi erat depicta figura Baffometi*.

They *honored* this symbolic image and often joined to their homage for their Baffomet their contempt for the cross of *Christ*.

We cannot question the truth of the secret ceremonies in use in the order of the Templars. To be convinced, it is sufficient to read the judicial information, and to compare it to the testimonies of the other knights of England, free and honorable men.

Voltaire and Abbé Millot,[42] who barely sees without Voltaire's eyes, don't want to totally admit that the Templars disowned Christ.

> "What would they have won," says Voltaire, "in damning a religion that fed them, and for which they fought?"

Singular manner to write the history of the human mind!

> "This golden head", pleasingly continues Voltaire, "mounted on four feet, *that they were alleged* to worship, and that was kept at Marseille, had to be presented to them [to the inquisition]. They simply did not look for it; and we must admit that such an accusation destroys itself." [43]

Voltaire was wrong, even on the name of the Grand Master of the order of the Templars. He calls him *Jean de Molay*. Millot corrected this mistake; but he stated with Voltaire that "the accusations for which one abolishes the order of the Templars shock all verisimilitude. How would it be possible that the novices were required to disown Christ?" exclaims Abbé Millot. Nice

---

[42] [SE: Abbé Claude Millot (1726-1785). A French historian expelled from the Jesuit order who published *Elements of the History of France*, *Elements of the History of England*, *Elements of Universal History*, *History of the Troubadours*, *Memoirs for the History of Lewis XIV and XV*, &c].

[43] [SE: Voltaire, *Essai sur les mœurs et l'esprit des nations*. Volume 1:9:66].

reflection, in truth, for a historian whose profession is to write some facts; probable or unlikely! There is an axiom in history:

"At times truth may not seem probable." [SE: Nicolas Boileau-Despréaux. L'Art poétique (1674)]

Certainly, the ceremonies of the Templars are strange; their *Baffomet* is an even stranger thing: but...
What could be the origin of so many honors to such a grotesque image? Could we discover a primary reason in the history of the opinions of the ancient world? In the customs and in the maxims of the Templars?
Jean Frederick Nicolaï, [44] *bookseller* in Berlin; as Richardson [45] was in England, is the first writer who thought about asking these questions, and who tried to answer them. Unhappy about the vague and contradictory assertions of all historians who copied Dupuy, [46] writing under the eye of the master, he suspected that the shy historian threw some veils maybe purposely on the *acts* that he had been entrusted with. And since opinions are only opinions, he studied the acts, always relying on the old and modern history; and verifying the Greek and Latin etymologies, he finally discovered in the acts and in the foreign testimonies, what not historian before him had seen there. His research announces an incredible penetration. There is probably a little bit too much dryness and embarrassment in his work. It is not without imperfections; but one can find nearly everywhere this strength of attention and this depth of perception that constitutes the true genius.
Here are roughly the results of his research. [47]
There was among the Templars an oral tradition, that assigned the origin of the abnegation of Christ's Divinity to a knight Templar, who had been made, one said, prisoner by the Saracens, and who had not received of them his liberty, unless if he were to disown Christ, and to introduce the use of it in his order. The thing is incredible and false, as we are going to ensure: but these hearsays indicate a trace that it is not necessary to leave slightly. In the

---

[44] [SE: Jean Frederick Nicolaï]
[45] [SE: Probably Samuel Richardson (1689-1761). English novelist and established stationer and printer.]
[46] [SE: Probably Pierre Dupuy (1582-1651). Illustrious French historian who became Guard of the Library of the King and Adviser at the Parliament. Among others books , he wrote *Traittez concernant l'histoire de France; sçavoir la condamnation des Templiers, avec quelques actes; l'histoire du Schisme, les papes tenans le siege in Avignon; et quelques procez criminels.* Paris, 1654.]
[47] *Versuch über die Tempelherren-Orden und das entitehen Freymaurergesellschaft.* 2 Vol. 8 Berlin 1782 der. [SE: Friedrich Nicolaï, *Versuch über die Beschuldigungen, welche dem Tempelherrn-Orden gemacht worden, und über dessen Geheimniß, etc.n V1-2 (1782)].

circumstanced confessions of the Templars, one finds a very important fact there to discover the reason of the introduction of this custom in the order.

"As the Templar denied Christ's Divinity, trampling his cross underfoot, he was also required to solemnly confess to a God All Mighty Creator of Heaven and Earth."

This religious confession evidently demonstrates that this abnegation of Christ was not the effect of an indecent or sacrilegious game, established with the intention of making an outrage to the true God that they worshiped: and far from being to their eyes a ceremony of blasphemy, one sees a respectful homage there to the Divinity. Were they wrong or right? This question doesn't concern me; I write some facts; and I demonstrate by facts that the real and unique goal of this ceremony was to confess to ONLY one GOD!

Now it is necessary to know that the belief in a *single* God was the fundamental doctrine of the religion of the Saracens or Muslims; the doctrine of a *Triple God* was inconceivable to the Saracens who went as far as calling it absurd. They did not want the worship of images and they blamed the Christians for having several Gods: one God the Father, equal to his Son, and God the Son as equal to his Father and without beginning as the God his Father; and the Holy Spirit, a third God equal to both. They were saying to the Christians, "If you honor in your divine Trinity something else than 'the three *principles* that came out from within the Eternal,' you are only idolaters. We are the only ones worshiping the true God, the unique God, and the Father of Nature!"

A similar religious zeal also animated the two parties: The Muslims called their war a holy war. It was the holy war of the Christians. A holy war that only produced the crimes and robberies setting fire to the East and the West. The great Saladin attacked in his states. Not expecting treaties of peace anymore, he first tried to spill terror in the camp of the crusaders: he had the prisoners slaughtered, and he especially pursued the Templars with great fury. However the first fire of the war soothed down little by little; both sides sent of deputies, truces and cessation for arms were suggested, and prisoners stopped being slaughtered. They learned to know one another better and the mutual esteem choked the violence of national hate. When a Templar was made prisoner, he was blamed ignominiously for worshiping several Gods; and he answered in vain: I was told since childhood that to be *saved* it is necessary to *believe* what the church believes. This was not an answer that could convince or refute a Muslim. The Templar himself, poorly educated, but often man of reason and good warrior, would let himself easily convinced that it was not necessary to worship several Gods. He would leave quite convinced by the Muslim that the popes were ambitious people who armed Europe only for the interests of Rome. He found on one hand a mystery that he could not conceive, and on the other the scheming that he understood very well: the Templar was rather embarrassed! Sometimes he would confess with loyalty that he didn't really see how three Gods in three people made only one and the same God!

This led for sure to decreasing even more and strongly the faltering respect of the Templars towards the *mystery* of the Trinity, these were the schisms of the Greek and Latin churches; and according to the expression of some historians, the *vagrant* ideas of the church on the doctrine of the divinity and of the two natures of Christ, so closely bound to his filial divinity, equal in the mystery to the Trinity to the divinity of the Father. These quarrels, of little importance in the practice of moral virtues, but of major interest in the *exercise* of faith and the submissiveness of the peoples towards the Roman clergy, gave birth everywhere to a myriad of sects, daring in their opinions; and progressively changing as the numerous Gnostic and Manichaean societies broke up. Most of these people rebelling against the commandments of the church worshiped the sun as the most beautiful image of the might of the Eternal.

They were far from preaching Christ's divinity, especially the Gnostics who bragged that he had been one of their brothers. This is a rather daring opinion, and it seems however that Milton adopted it in his regained paradise. He puts in the mouth of the Son of Mary a sublime and deep speech. The young child is indignant about the tyranny of the Romans and he intends to break the chains of his homeland. Furthermore, he wants to bring down the insolent audacity of the priesthood of these times. In his meditations, he penetrates in the thickness of a desolate wood; soon he cannot find his way anymore; he gets lost, and gets lost more and more in the desert, rolling in his heart past and future! Contemplation of a big hope, exclaims the Poet, quite capable to interest a *chosen society* in favor of a kind child:

> As well as might recommend
> Such solitude before choicest society.[48]

Now History teaches us that the Gnostic and Manichaean people, and the imprudent others who wanted to persist without the help of the popes, were all persecuted by the dominant church. Some were even burned for the edification of the faithful; and on the *year of grace*, etc. they were thrown in the flames "for the love of the Trinity and of their money." However their opinions were kept in secret and even spread and strengthen, as it is of use, as a reaction against the attacks and the cruelty of the persecutors. The theses of the Greek and Latin Churches on the mystery of the Trinity inflamed all minds during the twelfth and thirteenth centuries. These studies then universal often led to the doctrine of unity of God; and these Unitarians were persecuted again as the enemies of an avenging and merciless God jealous of his glory.

---

[48] Milton's *Paradise regained*. First Canto.

The monstrous usurpations of the popes, who had no shame to violate, in the name of a rightful God, the rights of nature and nations, made a large number become partisans of the opinions of persecuted ones!

One of the main reasons that spread the doctrine of the Saracens on the unity of God was their meetings with the Christians in the time of the crusades in the East. The conquests of the Moors in Spain had a major influence on the whole Europe; because then the Christians and the clergy were exhausted by ignorance and fanaticism; the flame of reason was nearly extinguished in Europe; the ancients were not studied any more, there were no more letters, no more artists, no more master pieces of art. [On the other hand] sciences and arts bloomed among the Saracens; they had rich libraries and scholarly academies in the East and in Spain. They established several schools that soon became famous. Their philosophy and their humanity made them cherished by losers as well as liberators and demigods. People would travel in Spain to have a closer understanding of them, to see them and to study them at their place. To participate in their research on the mysteries of nature, one learned their language, the Arab language. The study of a people's language necessarily leads to the knowledge of its religious principles and these Arabs, also known as Moors, Saracens, Muslims or Turcomans, had for fundamental dogma of their religion, the unity of God. Attempts were made to refute these armed and conquering Arabs but there was no knowledge on how to answer theological arguments with the weapons of reason. Soon these refutations in all Europe really came closer to the unity of God and the alarmed pontiffs feared the loss of their authority, damaged as soon as Europe would stop *believing* blindly. It even happened that numerous honest people outraged by the incredible abuses from the authority of the pontiffs and to escape their tyrannical orders; confessed publically the religion of Arabs. The robberies and crimes of the crusaders in the East, the most ferocious ones always being prelates, priests and monks, could only inspire horror for a bloody religion. Several among them loosing sight of the august mystery of the Trinity embraced the party of the Saracens which they could not prevent admiring and liking, seeing how these Saracens behaved, they said; *reasonably* and *honorably*!

Some authentic annals attest the close relationships between crusaders and Saracens. The light turcopole militia of the Saracens was composed of Saracens and Christians. The Christians also had their militia called pullani, also formed of Saracens or Mohammedans and of Christians.

During the truces, the Saracens and the crusaders had tournaments and games of war to practice fraternally the profession of arms. Christians in minor Asia made currency with the name and image of Mahomet; and the public history of these Crusades teaches us that the Templars permitted on their lands the religious cult established by Mahomet.

Emperor Frederick II, Richard Lion Heart, King of England, and the Templars also formed multiplying alliances with the Saracens. A last truce between Saladin and Richard signed for three years, three months, three days and three hours, solemn date that gives in total a number *twelve*, increased considerably the close relationships between Templars and Saracens. Both sides treated the prisoners well. The whole army of the crusaders finally perceived that the Saracens, in spite of the pontiffs who made them pass for monsters, were indeed, asides from their cult, learned and benevolent men.

A long absence from their homeland and from everything that was dear to them, fatigues, illnesses, famine and all calamities of the war had cooled little by little the zeal of the crusaders for the commands of the pontiffs. All leaders, often beaten, expressed at a time the desire to return to Europe. The ambitious Richard had to renounce the hope of his dreadful victories. Saladin was honored; admired and cherished even by the Christians.

Additionally, we note that there was a secret tradition among Templars whereby Saladin was received in their order by the knight Hugo of Tiberias[49] and that he fulfilled all the ceremonies of the order, except the *public reception* in the order; and probably the ceremony of kissing the medal of the professed.

In all the histories of our Europe where one had to triumph over pontifical opinions and censures, mention has been made of the tears of the Christians and Templars on the death of this great Saladin:

> "He was in truth a prince of great generosity and true courage; the last action of his life was again a noble example of wisdom and compliance to the laws of nature. During his illness which he knew to be incurable, he ordered the cloth, in which his corpse was intended to be wrapped up, to be carried through all the streets, and commanded the officer who bore this attendant of death, to exclaim with a loud voice, "Behold all that remains to the great Saladin, the Conqueror of Asia." His testimony is again a noble lesson of tolerance and humanity; he bequeathed alms for the poor, whether Jews, Christians, or Mohammedans, without distinction;[50] intending to prove by this fact that he thought until death that all men are brethren and that, to relieve them, we ought not to inquire what they believe, but what they endure.

---

[49] [SE: This is probably the Christian knight Hugh of Tiberias (not called Dodekin). The Saladin texts include the actual knighting of Saladin by his Christian teacher: thus Saladin receives the accolade and becomes himself a knight in the Occidental manner. See *Conjectures: medieval studies in honor of Douglas Kelly*. 1994. P. 91]

[50] See G. Vinifauf lib. VI [SE: Probably Vinifauf's account of the expedition of King Richard I to the Holy-Land. There is some uncertainty on the spelling of his last name, which appears to be Vinsauf. He used to be regarded as the author of *Itinerarium Regis Ricardi*, a narrative of the Third Crusade, but this is certainly false], and also Voltaire. *Essai sur les mœurs et l'esprit des Nations*. 1756. Vol. 2.

Who would not dare say of Saladin, although a Mohammedan, what Cicero said, while speaking of a *good* and *great* man?[51] One must believe that there has never been a good man, whom was supported by the looks of the Divinity: and there has never been a great man, who was not inspired, or *divinized* by a thought of the eternal."[52]

Finally moderation, beneficence and again science and healthy philosophy were nearly entirely on the side of the Saracens.

From what we made known of the relationships between crusaders and Saracens, and of Saladin's furies against the Templars, changed suddenly in kindliness and in brotherly devotion, it is at least probable than a Templar knight, prisoner in the East brought back, upon his return in the order, the great news that the Saracens believed in only one God! But we cannot reasonably believe that simply to please to the Saracens, and without any other motive, the Templars established in their order a new secret profession where it would be necessary to deny and to abjure Christ's divinity; abnegation in conformity with the oaths of the entire order, since it was its inner and mysterious doctrine: *Disciplina arcani.*

Add to this the fact that the Templars, when they trampled underfoot a crucified God, rendered great honors to an image that had the shape of a human head. The venerable image was only exposed in the most *secret* assemblies. Since the Mohammedans, in their religion, had images in horror, it is necessary to look *elsewhere* for the origin of the cult practiced by the Templars respectful of their mysterious image.

The name of this image, visibly foreign, since it doesn't have any sense in our modern languages, must help us discovering the origin of its cult. This symbolic image of the Templars, or to use the terms dedicated in the examinations, their *bearded* idol, was made figuring Baffomet, *in figuram Baffometi*; the judicial information attest to us that the *figure* of Baffomet was painted on this idol, *ubi erat depicta figura Baffometi.*

Since the Templars were taught during their reception to believe in a God Almighty, creator of heaven and earth and since the figure of Baffomet was then presented to their thoughts, it is indubitable that this name of *Baffomet*, name dedicated to the cult of the eternal, had to depict for them, through a visible sign, what the abstract words *Dio* and *Iddio*, or *Gott* or *God*, express today for the Spaniards, the Italians, the Germans and the English. It was the expression, the painting and the *image* of everything that one hears by the word *God.* In the Greek language, one finds at the word Baffomet a specific meaning that confirms this opinion resulting from the attested facts.

---

[51] Credendum est, neminem virorum bonorum talem fuisse nifi adjuvante deo. Et nemo unquam fuit vir magnus sine afflatu aliquo divino. Cicero. *De Natura Deorum.*

[52] This passage is extracted from a *Histoire de l'Europe moderne* (History of Modern Europe), currently under press [SE: This is probably Bonneville's work].

1. Scottish Masonry and Templars

The French word *Baffomet* doesn't come more evidently from the Latin word *Baffometus*, than the Latin *Baffo-Metus* doesn't derive immediately from the Greek words *Baphé-Métous*. This name, composed of two words, means literally *baptism of wisdom, dye of wisdom*. Now it is by *wisdom* that the Eternal dips itself in its works. The word baptism in Greek is in its turn the synonym of the words *purification* or *fertilization*. It also means allegorically life, the *life of wisdom*, of eternal wisdom, and therefore *eternal life*, the most beautiful work, the most beautiful image of the divinity![53]

And we observe that all literal and metaphorical versions of the Greek word *Baffé-Métous*, that is, *Baffo-Metus* and *Baffo-Met*, agree naturally with the worship of a *single* God. We understand then the *reason* of their symbolic image; and the other circumstances of the secret professions of the order of the Templars are explained by a real and motivated purpose: because one knows too much that *among the ancients*, there were dogmas that one didn't dare to confess publicly, because of the *dominant* religion; and that among others the belief in a single and unique God was the most violently persecuted. Does this seem strange today? All the better for the posterity!

It is because of the persecutions of the believers in a single God that the Gnostics, who only wanted to accept a *single* God, had for a long time among them a secret *dogma* and allegorical initiations of hidden opinions, *disciplinae arcani*. The name of the *Gnostics* is Greek: the verb *Gnosti* was the first word of the famous inscription of the Temple of the Sun:

"Gnosti Seauton" Know Thy Self.

While this temple is dedicated to the sun, it doesn't mean that the Gnostics worshiped the Sun. Because our Churches are *dedicated*, either to Saint Denis, who carried his head after his death, or to Saint Dominique, who instituted the holy Inquisition; or to Saint Nicodemus; or to other Saints of the Roman calendar; it certainly does not mean that the French worship as quite powerful Gods, the great saints who gave their name to our Churches.

The Gnostics named themselves the priests of the sun, for the same reason that our monks and Benedictines are generally called the priests of an abbey; priests of Saint Dennis, of Saint Germain l'Auxerrois, etc. etc. and not priests of God. However they don't worship the abbey; it is God that they pretend worshipping. If we were to put more clarity in the theological discussions, there would not be *so much gall in the heart of devout people*: or at least the consequences of their willful blindness would not be so dangerous for honest people.

The Greek name of the Gnostics allows us to search for the origin of their opinions among the Christians of minor Asia; in the Greek empire that was still subsisting; in other words at the same time as the Greek language, and

---

[53] [SE: There are numerous discussions on the etymology and meanings of Baffometus. None however mention the Latin *Metus*, the personification of fear.]

the philosophy of this language must have greatly influenced the Christians of the East.

If I am going to look for the origin of the Gnostic opinions within the Christianity of the East, it is because the ecclesiastical history teaches me that the Gnostics appeared in public during the establishment of Christianity: as if they had been its trunk, its flower and its fruit, according to the expressions of the partisans of Gnosticism. In the first century, after Jesus' birth, the new Platonic philosophy was in strong use among the Jews. This makes Boulanger say that Celsus, according to the account of Origen, blamed the son of Mary for having borrowed several of his dogmas from Plato. While it would be true according to S. Augustine, mentioned by Boulanger, that we find in Plato the beginning of the gospel of S. John, Boulanger is wrong to accuse the Nazarene of not being even a great man. This phenomenal erudite would have provided his century distinguished services, if he gave more attention in depicting things; and if he did not stay focused in showing his particular indignation.[54]

Oh Jesus, Son of Mary, a true God on earth, you will always be for me the son cherished of the eternal: sublime and deserved name that provided Milton some verses full of enthusiasm and majesty.

"The son of God I also am, or was!
And if I was, I am: relation stands!
All men are sons of God."[55]

The Platonic philosophy in use for a long time by the Jews or *Joviens* or Israelites, gave birth to the cabbala, *kabbalah*. This name is too much desecrated nowadays by a mysterious populace to give us a weak idea of the deep respects of the sages that carried with pride the name of kabbalists. This proves that the kabbalah, well understood at the time, contained a noble and pure philosophy, although symbolic; and not *mysterious*; because, once again, a *symbol* is not a *mystery*.

The kabbalists probably believed in a single God since they taught the dogma of unity of God. They also had an allegorical *image* to give some accurate ideas of his works and his essence. If they wanted to *paint* the divinity in an abstract manner, i.e. holding *Everything* within itself, they *depicted* it to their disciples by a hairless head. If they had to paint the *creative* and *fecundating* God, a *bearded* head expressed this creation and this *fecundation*. The hairless head also represented the *immutability*, nature and the *essence* of things. The *bearded* head, an eternally continued creation; and in general the perpetual perfection of the things that falls under our senses. Since they followed the law of the Jews they were not allowed to *make* some images, for fear that with time, that corrupts all, one didn't venture to worship them.

---

[54] See *Christianity unveiled*.
[55] *Paradise regained.* Book IV.

1. Scottish Masonry and Templars

Since all our ideas come from the senses and God not being a *bodily* being, it is obvious that one can never teach the dogma of a God without needing to bring closer some more or less imperfect *signs*. God is everything that matter is not, how daring is it to paint it with what matter is? The kabbalists not wanting to abandon the sublime dogma of a unity of God; and fearing the manufacture of the images that fall under the senses; believed to have reached directly to their goal by using *spiritual* images, images *in words*, to give to their disciples an idea less distant from the Omnipotence of the ETERNAL that the gospel named the *word*, the word par excellence.[56]

The Gnostics are born from the kabbalists. However soon after the establishment European Christianity, the name and the sect of the Gnostics vanished, as lost in the shadows. But the controversial works and the annals of our Europe indicate everywhere, up to the time of the Templars, the Gnostic principles over thousands of centuries and the divine *emanations* or principles. The partisans of mystical theology detached themselves of the Jewish law, and manufactured *material* images according to the images in *words* of the Gnostics. They said to their initiates that the one who worshiped the crucified, was still very low in the scale of beings, and therefore victim of thousands of centuries; that the one on the contrary who had enough clarity to be sure that a man could never be the God Almighty who had no beginning, had already reached the noblest level on the scale of beings, the state of man finally, and then he had the entire GNOSIN; it is the human science. Some supported that the worshiped Jesus of the pontiffs had only been a magician.[57] Another sect, the *Ophites*, that confessed a father, an uncreated God, saw itself persecuted by the Christians of west, and cursed the Galilean.

The Basilidians had two images: one was a *male* statue and the other a *female* statue. They honored these allegorical images. We are quite happy that the good Irenaeus made of the image of the Basilidians a Jupiter and a Minerva.[58] This great discovery teaches us that at least one of the statues had a beard; and that the other didn't have. Basilides, like Pythagoras, required his disciples to be silent for several years, five whole years, according to some writers, until they received the whole Gnosin, the whole *science of the initiation*. One only, among one thousand, was admitted in the sanctuary; and among ten thousand initiates, only two were accepted to participate in the whole revelation of all secrets pulled from nature.[59]

The Carpocratians taught during their initiations, that Christ chose, in his *twelve* disciples, some faithful friends to whom he had confided all

---

[56] Gospel according to St. John

[57] See again *La Gémar*, and the Histoire abrégée du Christianisme in Chap. III of the *Christ dévoilé*.

[58] [SE: See Irenaeus, *Against Heresies*. C. 180. Ch. XXIV. Doctrines of Saturninus and Basilides.]

[59] [SE: See W. Smith, *A Dictionary of Christian biography, literature, sects and doctrines*. 1877. Basilides. Pp. 268-281.]

knowledge that he had acquired in the temple of Isis, where he remained close to sixteen years, and practiced a practical study, of which he was given the theory during childhood, educated by the Egyptian priests; and because the most beneficial remedies are nearly all composed of a poison dose, they said that the great physician, in the name of humanity, forbid them to communicate the science of good and evil, that is, the art of healing, but to the virtuous men. They had a secret sign to recognize one another, a sign attested by the gospel according to them. It was according to Gnostic signs that the disciples recognized their master in Emmaus. Taking the other's hand in a certain manner required an answer, an expressive touch, and this several times, in the shape of questions and answers imperceptible to all spectators.[60]

The Basilidians, the Carpocratians and all Gnostic sects, had a image where was engraved the word ABRASAX. This word analyzed by the calculation of the letters of the Greek alphabet, used for numbers at the time, give for total the number 365. The Gnostic probably understood this as the yearly revolution of the sun, to remind all its kindness, and told every initiate: *You walk under the eye of Nature!*

We still have today quantities of beautiful stones where this word is engraved. While they could date from before or after the time of Basilides, these religious medals cannot be denied coming to us from the Gnostics. In the collection of Chiflet two prints of these stones are identified with the engraving of the word ABRASAX.[61]

One of these stones displays the GNOSTIC, the SAVANT par excellence.

The great Worker of the eternity, the Father of the Gnostics, or in modern language the Creator and the Architect of the Universe, was represented on the stone with a long beard and long hair, to depict the order and the graces of creation. The Pythagorean pentagon, or five pointed star, was again on the chest of the venerable image. The emblem was said to be that of the Almighty's paternal conservation, because, according to the disciples of Pythagoras, his pentagon printed on the chest was a sign of acceptance; they called it the Pentagon of health and prosperity. The image also displayed the Gnostic *ogdoad*, an eight pointed *star*. The big star represented the Creator and the seven small stars represented the emblem of the seven *emanations* of the Omnipotence!

The whole system of the priests of the sun is linked with the bearded and hairless image of the Templars. During their secret reception they were taught to believe in a single God, creator of the universe. And we prove that

---

[60] This Gnostic practice is presumably the origin of the usage, nearly universal in England, to always present the bare hand one meeting someone. An Englishman who was one day very hurried, told me, while giving me his gloved hand: "Excuse my glove".

[61] [SE: The word Abrasax ((Αβρασαξ)) was engraved on certain antique gemstones called Abraxas stones. A particularly fine example was included as part of the Thetford treasure from fourth century Norfolk, UK.]

they wanted to depict the image of the Creator of the Universe with their *Baffometus.* The hierophant who symbolized the God *visible through his kindness*, pronounced the Arab word Y Alla! God, or *light* of God![62] After the *Fiat lux*, or *granting of the light*, the grand master, while receiving the initiate to the degree of the brethren, said loudly, "This is God's friend! There is your beloved Son!" The Judges who interrogated the Templars consigned in their information the reproaches that they had against them for believing that the earth and the plants could germinate, bloom and ripen by the power of Baffomet: irrefutable proof that the Templars who believed in a single God, let us not forget it, saw in their *Baffomet* only the emblem and the image of the works of the Creator.

This dogma of the unity of God had always been for the Gnostics an allegorical revelation. And since it was said that the Son of Mary had been only one of their peers, and no the All Mighty God, this *secret* initiation for the Gnostics, had to be much more secret for the Templars. The mare suspicion of this belief would have sent them to tortures and to the stakes.

I don't see how I could refuse to believe that they associated a political goal to their sparse third and last profession. This military order, and these knights, roaming in the deserts of minor Asia needed a brotherly sign to insure that those *who knew how to pronounce it* were instructed of the biggest secret of the order, and that one could confide in them without danger.

The image of the Templars, where the face of the Baphe-Metous was painted, *image* of the *baptism* or *tincture of wisdom*, was therefore *evidently* the symbol of the Creator's works. But did the real meaning of the *baptismal sign* painted within the bearded and hairless image remain? In other words, was there a defined meaning to indicate the form that one had to use during the initiation of the *baptism of wisdom*? Was it an *algebraic* or *geometric* figure?

It was however a Greek figure and a sign of *initiation*. We saw that the pentagon or the Pythagorean star was a sign of acceptance. To dare to pronounce what was the same sign, would be foolhardiness.

But Nicolaï appears so courageous to me in his research, and so wise in his observations, that I cannot disagree with him. What would further lead me to believe in this analogy, as sufficiently proved, it is that the *Blazing Star*, found on the *engraved* tracing boards of the first carpet of the English Freemasons is a *pentagon*, a five pointed star *figure*.

This allegory probably deserves to be studied. We know the respect of the seven sages for the *star pentagon*.

The Ophites, who painted in *allegorical words* their ideas on Nature and on the Divinity, said *in their symbols*:

> "The souls, while returning to *God*, must show the signs of their purification on earth to the ARXONTAS, the *Masters*."

---

[62] [SE: "Yalla" - "Lets Go." "Y'Allah" - "Oh, God", origin of the Spanish "Ole".]

How do we explain this allegory? While its literal meaning is absurd to me, I know that these words were respected by wise men. Then, they must contain a hidden meaning...

I clearly recognize in these *Archontes,* or rulers, the judges of the Greek hell, the guardians of the Elysian Fields, the dragons watching over the Garden of the Hesperides. These Archontes, who watch over at the gate of the heavenly regions,[63] may have some remote relationship with the Apostle who was said to be entrusted with the keys to Paradise by Jesus. *These cross-shaped keys.*

But some uncertain research would bring me away from my topic. I allow with all my heart scholars to compare the Archontes to the Apostles and the symbols of the Ophites to their symbols. They can even make these Archontes the *tylers* at the entrance of the holy temple of the great Architect of the Universe. However, the prayers of the Ophites are indubitable. They had to pronounce them when they were presented with the *image in words*, or the *parabola* that I have just mentioned. Now this *verbal image* could very well be the parabola of the Pythagorean pentagon; or the five-pointed star, figured by spiritual allegory. This would be in conformity with the dogmas of the Gnostics and the Ophites were a branch of it either entrenched or an off-shot to probe the field, the spirit and the customs of the time.

The prayers of the Ophites in the presence of the sacred pentagon further prove that this Pentagon was the sign of their initiation. So the relationship between the Templars and the Gnostics is demonstrated.

We conceive easily their participation in the initiation of the *Baffomet* or *baptism of wisdom*, allowed them to think without fright of damnation that they did not need any blessings and absolutions of the pope's ministers whom they perceived as hypocrites or suckers.

After having exposed in this way the whole secret of the order of the Templars, we now have to compare the order of the Templars with the all modern institution of the *free and accepted* Masons.

This is where the invisible authority of these nice Supérieur Inconnus is found *legal* and cherished. They *mysteriously* try, via public criers, to spread, among the populace of Europe that they hold *a secret to make gold*, as successors of the Templars.

Thousands of times the free and accepted Masons were warned as brethren not to believe in impostors, who announce *foreign* gods; who argue between them the right to deceive the weak minds and, in a word, who arm them as brigands. In England the *Scottish* dagger has already been banned.

Nothing stops the *bluebeard* Superior; they write mysteriously under the coat of anonymity and speak with incredible effrontery. If we were to listen to them, the public history is false; nothing is *true* but what is within their private discussions.

---

[63] [SE: séjour d'élection.]

1. Scottish Masonry and Templars

These good Superior *Inconnus,* putting no restrains to their impertinent assertions, contradict one another every day, they are compelled to prove that we waited a long time to tear the veil covering them. As long as they have been the subject of the public execration, it would have been quite barbarian to reject them from a brotherly asylum where they had slipped themselves in by putting on the mask. At the time they didn't compare Saint Ignatius to Caesar and Saint Xavier to Alexander: in very little time these invisible Gentlemen finally succeeded in preparing them thousands of worshippers.

The columns are raised, the temple is built. The *number* of the sanctuary is engraved. One waits for this explanation: and they wait in turn for the moment to give it. And they sleep quite peacefully. But they were granted so many innovations, they have so much voice at the chapter, and they write so gorgeously that it is necessary to explain to them once and *for all* what they should have read a long time ago in the Sanctuary of Tolerance and Truth.

> "A *beneficent* genius always has kept an eye on this house, because it was the home of a holly Man."[64]

Here is a tolerance of about one century! It is quite excusable today to hand the bloodthirsty priests over to the *public indignation.* To further wait would have required handing them over to the secular arm. The choice is clear because the philosopher only wants reason for weapon and his battle cry is *humanity.* They don't know how to argue except in having the honor to add *more light* to the light of reason, and also the happiness to serve TRUTH with an audacious zeal.

In England I was revealed the whole code of Jesuitism, including the intention to make it public; an undertaking that became more dangerous by the day. People were looking for the feather and the heart of a French to speak a European language, a human Language!

Some Masonic speeches pronounced in the lodges of England, where my determination to enter into Masonry was slightly forced,[65] and the ESSAYS of my first youth, and the honor to be French, inspired some confidence in my zeal!

I locked myself in with my titles; I verified everything, compared everything, and analyzed everything. To convince myself about the Jesuitic codes, I used all efforts of my reason. When the scheming of the Jesuits appeared to me demonstrated as clearly as my own existence, I didn't hesitate anymore.

Poor blinds! Tear your headband! First of all, quickly leave the sanctuary of the false Gods! May these gods themselves leave it!

---

[64] The Sun God in Euripides' *Alcestis.*

[65] [SE: Bonneville was initiated in England in 1786.]

I embraced the column of the temple of the false gods: I already feel that my weak hand is sufficient for its ruin. It will be dethroned.

I only want to bury their daggers; under the ruins of a temple built towards Imposture.

Religious and entirely Gnostic principles made the great secret of the Templars in the fourteenth century: and the first principle of free and accepted Masons is that, *as they say*, religion is not at all their object. The immediate relationship of this modern society with the former order of the Templars is therefore only a chimera. The principles of a secret society can endure major changes, infinite modifications; but it is not possible that these principles become contradictory.

The free and accepted Masons have allegorical ceremonies, and the Templars had allegorical ceremonies: This does not prove that the symbols of these two orders are the same. We showed that they didn't look alike.

The third profession of the Templars was the last initiation. It was there that the secret of the order was confided.

Now no Scottish or *clerical* degrees confide a secret to the initiates: the only one given to them is an alleged immediate relationship with the Templars: this is a lie. It cannot be the *secret* of the society since the degrees assert that the revelation of the complete history of the Inner Sanctuary would not betray the secret of the Scottish Masters.

For Templars, the goal of the order was to remove the power from the priests: For free and accepted Masons, everything is about preparing the OMNIPOTENCE of the unmarried priests and the delirium of superstition. Some were running into danger to defend the widow and the orphan; here absurd pretensions are established on the chimerical rights of an order punished [too cruelly probably!] for its insolence; greed and emerging despotism. The Templars disowned the divinity of Jesus and this was a political secret. The free and accepted Masons certainly don't have to reveal such a secret on the *altar of the All Mighty*.

Would they ever dare say (what are they not capable of?) that their *blue* apron represents the *belt* of the order of the Templars, that the cord of election with three times three knots given in some lodges to the Scottish Masters represents the *secret belt* of the Templars, that the image of a *dead* in his coffin, and this is the august ceremony of the highest degree of Scottish Masonry, is the emblem of the Baffometus of the Templars. Even here there would no allegorical similarity or immediate relationship with the order of the Templars.

A Templar *testified* under the terms of the *testimony* that a small number of Templars, probably some elders of the last initiation, carried in their journeys *in their chests* the image of Baffomet. We could say as much about the image of the Scottish masters carried by a few of them in their journeys: but this image doesn't look like the Baffomet of the Templars.

This image, what image! is a cadaver in a coffin. His head is that of a young and robust man. His two arms are crossed on his chest. The body of the cadaver is in a purple shroud. This shroud is a kind of blouse or sacerdotal chasuble that goes down to the middle of the thighs. From the elbow, the arms and the hands of the cadaver are naked. He carries on the left arm, above the elbow, and on the purple shroud a *red* cross. In some lodges of this high degree the cadaver has an injury on his forehead. In some others, where the forehead of the cadaver does not appear to have been wounded, it is easy to see that the head had first been cut and then united back to the trunk. In some instances, it is about *Saint John Baptist*, in some others it is about the Grand Master *Molay* and sometimes it is about *Christ*.

The highest *light* of a happy initiate to this degree of degrees is to know how to say:

"This corpse is the image of *a man* who was *buried* in a country where one would look for him the least; and he can still be seen there today."

This allegory is provided with so many secrets and solemnity that good people who love life dearly, which is rather natural, forget for a moment the *necessity of the laws of nature*. I knew some who were quite convinced that if their head was cut, the Superior Inconnus would have, if they deemed it appropriate, a sure method to put it back on as if it was a broken leg: oh delirium of the human mind!

This allegory cannot depict such secret, since it is impossible. It is simply the allegory of the order of Jesuits.

The young man is the order: he is painted young, because the order of the Jesuits didn't exist in the ancient world; he is painted robust because, as we know, the order previously had untiring members, and that it still has many partisans. To be convinced of this, we only have to open the recently published *Travels* of Baron of Riesbeck. This is a very curious work where *specters appear* to princes hostile to Jesuits; and princes, who suddenly pierce a *Spanish dagger* through the body of these specters, unfortunately killing their confessor.[66]

Sometimes, the young man has an injury on the forehead: it is a dangerous stroke carried to the order: Often, we see that the head of the young man has been cut; we know that the Jesuits have been hunted down everywhere *with their miracles*; that they deserved the name of *scourges of mankind*, and that finally the order was decapitated. But it is indeed the head of the hydra of the swamps of Lerna; the monster picked up its head and tried to put it back on the dismembered body, dragged in the sludge and dispersed in the deserts. The Superior Inconnus assure that the *young man* still lives where

---

[66] *Travels of Baron of Riesbeck*, 3 Vol. Paris, 1783, at Buisson [SE: Riesbeck's work appeared in German in 1783 and was translated into English as *Travels through Germany, in a series of Letters* by P. H. Maty, in 1787. A French version translated from English by Le Tourneur, *Voyage en Allemagne, dans une suite de lettres*, also appeared in 1787.].

we would suspect it less: it is the order that stands up again, hidden under a Masonic veil; there is this Grand Master that lives *again* and ask the help of the Scottish Masters.

This Jesuitical allegory becomes even clearer through the emblems of the Jesuitical books published on Masonry.

They like so much to depict *exactly* the misfortunes and the triumphs of their order, that their *preachers*, in the splendor of the Jesuitism (as for example, when they succeeded in seducing the great king, the generous Louis XIV, to revoke the Edict of Nantes), painted the sun in all its glory.

The sun is the image that the Jesuits took modestly as emblem of their order. When the order was a bit harassed, when it was banished for the crimes unimaginable to those who did not study their history, they painted the *sun* at its sunset. At the days of the triumph of the order, they painted the *moon* eclipsed by the sun.

The moon is for the Jesuits the emblem of Masonry. When the order was abhorred and hunted down, they painted the *moon* in its full, and the sun was hidden under the horizon. Shy star and full of modesty, oh moon! Oh restful torch of the nights! Soft light of the sensitive souls, would your purpose have come to be only that of *shedding light* on the attacks of the brigands!

In the sixteenth century, the Jesuits were powerful. With the help of the auricular confession, this order knew the politics of the sovereigns and the secret of the families: Any society or fraternity made them fear some rivals; it was eradicated, or soon, after having seduced or dispersed the leaders, they gave him an alchemical armor. It was the universal passion of the century; all princes of Europe had their astrologers and their alchemists.[67]

In those times, an impostor gave himself a crowd of ridiculous names to make himself a laughing stock to the silly, who are, as one knows, the biggest number, He took advantage of his luck to heal several illnesses, with remedies then very extraordinary: he used opium and mercury. Is he the author of this discovery? Scholars have serious reasons to doubt this. However they have not doubts that he became used to claim as his the inventions of others. He took from a modest philosopher[68] a singular idea;

---

[67] See *La Fama* of Jean-Valentin *Andreae*, printed in 1614; his *Assertion*, also printed in 1614, and his *Mythologia Christiana*, published in 1618. See the *Symbola Aurea Mensoe*, of Michel Mayer (or Maier); his *Atalanta Fugiens*; his *Thémis Auréa*. See also the *Summum Bonum*, of Robert Fludd; and have a look, if you dare, on the horrible *in-folio* of this Englishman, who was not a man without merits.

[68] Isaac Hollandus. [SE: The writings of Johann Isaac Hollandus and his son Isaac Hollandus and their writings have been sources of discussions. At time, the Hollandus have been sought to be fictitious. Their writings were originally thought to date back from the fifteenth century and this was used by anti-Paracelsus (Aureolus Theophrastus Bombast) factions to blame him of plagiarism. Another opinion suggests that these works date from the last

that salt, sulfur and mercury were the principles of things; and he roamed the crossroads shouting.

> "I compose salt, sulphur and mercury;
> There is my trinity, the soul of nature."

This Aureolus Theophrastus *Bombast* was a small knight of industry, who, talking about precious remedies, sympathy and magic like a boaster, had arrived, in spite of his depraved morals, to make for himself among the populace, a great reputation of healer.

Of all sovereigns of the century, Rudolph II contributed the most to spread the reputation of the secret arts. By mistake he also laid the foundations of this horrible superstition of the seventeenth century. It was at Rudolph's court that the mysterious impostors ran in crowd: Tycho Brahe, who compared fortunately the seven planets from the *heaven* to the seven planets of the crucible, was royally rewarded. Rudolph also invited to his court the famous John Dee, English chemist, who had dedicated his *Hieroglyphic Monad* to the Maximilian emperor.

This *Hieroglyphic Monad* of the English chemist was a figure where the *sun*, the *moon*, *mercury* and a *cross* were united.[69]

The extravagant expenses of Rudolph and the honors that were rendered at his court to all these impostors, made a lot of the noise in Europe: those were only the *visible* results of the enormous expenses of the emperor and the work of his protégés. The partisans multiplied. The Jesuits, whose religious scheming and flexibility depicted the so well by Pascal in his *Letters*, and Racine in the priest of his *Athalie*, favored the emperor's tendencies and weaknesses, to divert him from his government's functions.

Already the Jesuits governed despotically the two branches of the house of Austria in the empire and in Spain. There would be misfortune against the one who dared raise the voice against their despotism; he would always be a villain to deliver to the executioners. If they had no pretext to impute to him the appearance of a crime, they would call him impudently by the name of his country, like an odious name to the All Mighty! A resident of Albi was an *Albigensian*; this strange name was for the people the synonym of brigand or

---

part of the sixteenth century and that they drew their ideas from Paracelsus, rather than the opposite.]

[69] *Monas Hieroglyphica, by John Dee,* 1569. This John Dee is also the author of the *Fasciculus Chemicus*, or Chymical Collections [SE: It appears that the *Fasculus Chemicus* was written by his son Arthur Dee], and of another work that has never been printed, whose existence however is certain by the quotes of the contemporary authors. This work had for title NAOMETRIA, or, Mercury of the Vessel, Measure of the Temple. This is why this John Dee, true impostor, was so famous among so many initiates *masoned* by the Jesuits [SE: It appears that the *Naometria* was written by Simon Studion and not John Dee].

heretic! If some philosopher dared blaming them for their innovations in the discipline of Christ, they immediately accused him of atheism and heresy: if he dared *to protest* his innocence, they called him a *protestant*. They made the populace hate this name alone and being called as such was a forfeit worthy of death: they were burned by hundreds, while the *Veni Sancte Spiritus* was song!

A religion instituted by God himself could not order the cruelty; there was a rising of a crowd of honest people who believed that our holly religion was abominable; specific associations were formed in Austria, in Bohemia and in Hungary; a particular cult was created based on rather misunderstood Gnostic principles; but since it included all the fraternal and cordial aspects of the mystic theology as found in Thomas à Kempis, it did not lack senators.[70]

How can we wonder after this, that the rests of these *Protestants* of the sixteenth century did not want to abandon a beneficent hierarchy that advocated popular education for some spouses, for the children who will be fathers and for the fathers of families?[71]

The assemblies of the partisans of *Protestantism* had to be secret. Their speeches and their works had a mysterious style that was then only meaningful to their brothers, therefore they named themselves:

"Brothers in Christ" they said one to the other "let us seriously focus on Christ and never on the external."

These words were obscure, and offered no meaning that could displease the Jesuit persecutors: but they were meaningful for the Albigensians, the Bogomils, the Gnostics, the Ophites, the Lutherans, the Calvinists and so many other Protestant *families*: My brethren, let's lend an attentive ear to the voice of the inner oracle. It is the voice of conscience which is Christ's voice. For them, the *external* things meant the orders of the pontiffs and all their interpretations of the Scripture that seemed to wound reason or humanity.

However, they fell on all sides under the blade of the Jesuit persecutors and executioners: the outraged France drove the Jesuits out: but they had to go against Germany and Spain where all sovereigns were the submitted slaves of the Jesuits: France called the Jesuits back but they were hunted down in England where they tried in vain to come.

The emperor Ferdinand I, governed by the scheming of the Jesuits, showed himself as cruel and intolerant towards his own subjects. One had in execration a temple where the Jesuits spilled their poisons and their hate; one embraced in a jumble the scattered principles of Gnosticism and the

---

[70] See *The Imitation of Christ*, by Thomas à Kempis.

[71] [SE: "... I tell you we must everywhere have schools for our boys and girls, to the end that the man shall be fit for his duties and the woman for directing her household and rearing in a Christian way, her children." *Libellus de instituendis pueris; magistratibus et senatoribus civitatum Germanioe Martinus Luther.* Marthin Luther. 1521.]

fraternity of the mystical cult: the princes of Germany hastened to form a league against the house of Austria that decided to bend them under the scepter of the Jesuits.

Henry IV, as a good King, and only by humanity, offered help to the Protestants: he even suggested taking arms with them against the house of Austria. He protected all the princes of Germany, persecuted by the Jesuits under a pretext of religion. Under the safeguard of an entire people's genius, and of a French people of which he was the worshiped king, Henri IV could not escape the dagger of the Jesuits.[72]

The goal of the Jesuits was to eradicate on the earth all principle of research concerning religion, that is to say, all matter that could offend them. They were set to start by raising the pope above all kings, so long as he was always the work of their dreadful sanctuary, then a volcanic underground where were forged according to their orders the bulls and the thunderbolt of a Jupiter.

Bacon de Verulam was Lord Chancellor of England. He fed from all the wisdom of the ancients. Friend of the sciences and arts, and wanting to swarm the whole Europe of the ridiculous sects, the philosopher and minister

---

[72] Rousseau observed somewhere that the good Henry, *he deserved this name well*, is the only French king who was not elevated by a priest.

"Our priests, don't stop shouting against the non-believers and the philosophers, whom they treat as dangerous subjects. However when we open history, we never find that philosophers caused revolutions in the states: but on the other hand we don't see any revolution where people of the church were not part of. The Dominican who poisoned the emperor Henry VI *in a wafer*, Jacques Clément, Ravaillac were not non-believers, they were not philosophers: these were fanatic Christians who led Charles I to the scaffold." Boulanger. *Christianisme dévoilé* ("Christianity Unveiled") [Chapter 16. Conclusion].

"There is no Christian who not is taught, since childhood, that he is worth to obey God better than men: but to obey God is never to obey to the priests. God himself *doesn't speak anymore*; it is the *church* that speaks for him; and the church is a body of priests that often finds *in the Bible* that the Sovereigns are wrong; that the laws are criminal; that the most judicious establishments are impious; that tolerance is a crime, etc. Any sovereign that will have courage to think for himself, will feel that his power will always be shaky and precarious, as log as it will have support only in the ghosts of the religion, the mistakes of the peoples, and the caprices of the priesthood." Boulanger. *Christianisme dévoilé* ("Christianity Unveiled") [Chapter 11. Of Christian Morality].

This is how the philosophers write. But for fear that the people knows their works and gain knowledge from them, the priests make these blasphemies burn by an executioner's hand. If heaven gives to the earth some good king who is not their slave, they murder him.

of a powerful people, took great importance in the happiness of the human kind.

After having been the *New Instrument*[73] of the sages and the scholars of the ancient world; he published, under the form of a summery, a crowd of ideas on the art of gathering and enriching the deposit of the knowledge. To comply with the taste of the century that cherished allegories he published his work in the shape of novel. It was an unknown island, another Atlantis that he had discovered.[74] He speaks there of a literary society under the allegorical name of *Salomon's House*. He had the modesty to call his *Atlantis* an *unfinished work*: and the philosopher probably didn't expect that one would take *to the letter* the truth he had published under the allegorical meaning.

It is sufficient to open Bacon at random, to feel that he took pleasure to speak only by images and by symbols.

I will say more, his poet's eye, his genius made to create all effects of a beam of light thrown in the abyss of the human heart, always felt the irresistible need to leave to the thought its measure; it was therefore always the infinity to which het feared to give some boundaries; he saw *everything*, he wanted to paint *everything*: some of his images can leave you dreaming for ten whole days. These are not words *brought back* by a cultivated and highly intelligent person; they are beams of luminous ideas, of which all faces *reflect* a new world.

Bacon had prepared everything for a society of Naturalist sages. He was Prime Minister of a nation friend of the Sciences and Arts. One saw in England the creation of a society of Rosicrucians based on the ideas of the *New Atlantis*. Their symbols; nearly all Gnostic, *had to be*, as in the ancient world, the symbol of the universal harmony that unites man to man, and the man-God to the universe.

Among others symbols, these Rosicrucians had on a carpet the sun, the moon; the compass, the square [tool], the square [shape], the triangle, the sphere and a five-pointed star, that represented mercury for them.

To represent their first symbol more clearly, they painted it *flaming*. Mercury or quicksilver was, following their opinion, the ARCHAIOS, or *celestial fire*, or in other words, the *Holy Spirit*; and again more literally, the *mind*, or the *healing balm*; poured from the hands of the eternal *through all Nature*.

This opinion, misunderstood, was the reason of all *hermetic dreaming*. These Rosicrucians also spoke of journeys, of *moist* air and of *rain* etc. As for their metaphysical ideas, they were very very clear:

> "Matter", they said, "is out of God, and consequently bad: God is therefore the purest Spirit or the purest *Light*."

---

[73] See the *Novum Organum*.
[74] See the *Nova Atlantis* [New Atlantis].

1. Scottish Masonry and Templars

My goal is not to give a complete history of the origin of the symbols of the Society of the Rose-Cross; one finds the same symbols and even the name of Rose-Cross in *Christian Mythology*, printed in 1618.[75] It was not therefore precisely according to the ideas of Bacon of Verulam, that the English Society of the Rose-Cross was created.

Bacon was called the BRAHMIN of the North. I will uphold this name of Brahmin, or *interpreter of the mysteries of nature*, to mark, while we are here, the goal of the society. The symbols and the ceremonies of the Society of Bacon could be public, but it was necessary to hold secret the science of good and bad, that is to say, the interpretation of the allegories that was reserved to the new Brahmins.[76]

There were requirements of research on the conduct and morals, and on the intelligence of any person who wanted to be admitted there. I laid down some principles, I mentioned some facts; I didn't always believe necessary to draw all consequences from a fact; I often made do with drawing the attention there.

Rather the brotherly society of the Rose-Cross, or Brahmins of the North, is old or modern it is not the object of my work: All I need here is to show in the public history the birth or rebirth of the Society of the Rose-Cross. The carpet of our Freemasons, engraved *everywhere*, is similar to the carpet of these Rosicrucians, that has been kept to us by Valentin and others[77] The English took for model the Salomon house of Bacon; and today's Rosicrucians, a wild branch of the first Rosicrucians of England, still call their assemblies the *Solomonic Science*.

Charles I, king of England, who wanted to achieve the ideas of the *New Atlantis* was prevented to do so by the civil wars: however the compelling idea of Bacon for men devoured by the need to know had a great success in England in spite of the inner disturbances.

In 1646 some scholars began to assemble regularly; and their assemblies led to the birth of the Royal Society of Sciences in London: it was not entirely in conformity with the wishes of the Rosicrucians: They did not see it as modest enough, brotherly enough and serious enough.

The same year they established a new Rose-Cross society: the goal of this regeneration was to come closer to the ideas of the great Brahmin, and to remain modestly as unknown as his *island of Bensalem*. Their carpet displayed the ancient columns where it is said that Hermes had engraved the *elements* of sciences. Seven degrees led up to a *squared theater* which displayed *some symbols* on the creation: the study of nature was the unique object of the Solomon House.

I ask here great attention: it is the time of the birth of the name of Freemasons in the public history.

---

[75] [SE: Johann Valentin Andreae. *Christian Mythology*. 1618]

[76] See the *Atlantis* of Bacon.

[77] See *Christian Mythology*, 1618.

Everything that is found today on the carpets of Freemasons is borrowed from the carpet of the Rosicrucians or Brahmins of the North: the allegories *in words* are there the same; among our Freemasons *rain is contrary to light*, and *light is found through the travels.*[78]

But the Rosicrucian disciples of Bacon only had one carpet, only one grade; there was nothing secret with them except their *signs* of brotherly association. The *symbols* could be printed and given to everyone, but to *publish* the discoveries of the Society required its agreement: nothing wiser. One can call with Bacon the Solomon House the most useful establishment that there is in the world.[79]

Why is it that today's Masonry has so many multiplied degrees in Masonry, so many tests to see nothing of the allegories. Those of the first degree are printed in numerous works of the sixteenth century; they are found again with some modifications, admitted by some as *modern*, within the sanctuary: however they are also publicly printed.

Terrifying tests and horrible oaths are required in order to not reveal what is printed everywhere!

One believes himself a Templar, and one is silent; one boasts of this immediate relationship: it is sufficiently proven that in spite of severe mistakes the Templar knights were in general men of honor; one waits with readiness for their recall:

All this is natural and generous, one suffers in silence: one sees with pleasure the number of brethren increase; it is always a new suffrage, for the triumph of the order... of the order of the Jesuits!

We have presented all the contradictions of an alleged system of the immediate relationship of the Scottish Masters with the order of the Templars. Let us now present the obvious resemblance of the *four masonic degrees* of the thousands of lodges dedicated to Saint John with the four degrees or professions of the company of Saint Ignatius.

End of the first Part.

---

[78] See the Échelle des êtres in the *Contemplation de la Nature* by Charles Bonnet.

[79] See Nove ATLANTIS.

1. Scottish Masonry and Templars

2.

Similarity of the Four Oaths of the Company of Saint Ignatius and of the Four Degrees of the Masonry of Saint John.

Orient de Londres
1788

"People would go successively through the four degrees or four receptions and leave the temple as blind as they came in. And the golden veal that they incensed and worshiped and canonized was soon no more that a poor wretch, a god without gilding, a veal without silver thrown to rubbish." Part 2. Page 114

Introduction

Οὐ γὰρ ἂν μακρὰν

ἴχνευον αὐτός, μὴ οὐκ ἔχων τι σύμβολον

If I was not given good clues,
I would not have attempted *such* research.
Oedipus in Sophocles. *Tragoed.*[80]

"Tyranny has wrapped us in the darkness of ignorance. It may thicken this darkness but from time to time some explosions of light illuminate its impure clouds. These explosions of light announce to the wicked man that thunderbolts accumulate somewhere to make a great example of him. Touched by this, the earth will come out of the lethargic sleep where it dived, and like the sleepy taurus already searched by the poisons of the reptiles that believed it dead, the earth will shake its old bones, and will throw, I don't know where, the insects that dishonor it. "

Letter of N. of B. to Mr. the Marquis of Condorcet. London. 1786[81]

---

[80] [SE: "for I should not have traced it far, if I had attempted it by myself without any clue."] Sophocles, Oedipus-king. Scene 3.

[81] [SE: Nicolas de Condorcet was a central figure in the Enlightenment. He was a collaborator of de Bonneville in the late 16th century when de Bonneville and Claude Fauchet maintained the Society of the Friends of Truth and its reports. The works of de Condorcet were also published through the Cercle publishing house directed principally by de Bonneville.]

2. Masonry and Company of Jesus

Similarities of the Four Oaths and Four Degrees

When we read Jesuit works on Masonry, on the importance of its ancient mysteries and on the origin and on the progress of this order; we first imagine that they only wanted to entertain some readers with dreams and with innocent madness: but if we are lucky enough to study these works with the help of the code of the elected, we clearly see that it is about nothing less than overturning empires, and maintaining a catalyst of discord.[82]

The society of Masons is composed today of several millions of men and the number of initiates grows every day. It is a phenomenon in the history of the human mind! It seems to me that this society deserves more attention than to become incorporated in it and after that to start *working* with the majority! We know how the majority of Masons works!

So that all Masons work in the future as it suits to men, they must first acquire a Jesuitical *master key*; they need the courage to follow us in the most disgusting details. We will make these details as clear and exciting as possible!

It is within the history of our Europe that we will choose all our proofs. *Fiat lux*, let's shed a light on humanity.

The society of Rosicrucians, or disciples of Bacon, included *Elie Ashmole* who later on made himself famous as *antiquarian*.

This Elie Ashmole and a few other members of the brotherly society belonged at the same time to the *guild of Master Masons of England*: this circumstance of their inspection or direction or grand mastery of the *profession* of Masons served to provide them without expenses a convenient place for their assemblies of Rosicrucians. These Rosicrucians met in the

---

[82] See Smith, p. 241

2. Masonry and Company of Jesus

hall of the guild of Masons that assembled then and still today, like all others professional bodies several times a year.[83]

To leave no indication of their assemblies, the Rosicrucians who were not from the body of Masons, gained admission as the others in this guild of operative Masons.[84]

And to be distinct from the operative masons, they called themselves *free and accepted* Masons.

These Rosicrucian assemblies worried the Jesuits, *for whom nothing was hidden*: They tried to introduce themselves into it in a rather large number at a time of civil wars, during which the Rosicrucians rarely assembled. They easily dispersed the good ones who avoided all tumultuous assemblies and they gained some followers. Finally they succeeded in being the masters of it.

In 1682 the Jesuits formed a new system of FREE-MASONRY from the *Rose Cross* system of FREE-MASONS.[85] They transformed the Solomon *House* of Bacon into a *temple* of Solomon: they bent all symbols to their intentions and as a result of giving them some bizarre explanations, of which the Jesuitical meaning was reserved to their conspirators, they infected the purest source. Soon it was no more than a stagnant water from where pestilence would fly everywhere.

Let's show the exact correspondence and a complete relationship between the four degrees of the society of the Rose-Cross *Masoned* by the Jesuits and the four degrees of the order of the Jesuits.

In Maryland, in America and in Mohilow in Russia, there are still today four kinds of Jesuits, that is, there are four different Jesuit degrees:

The first-degree Jesuit is the lay brother or temporal, *temporalis* – T –.

The second-degree Jesuit is the *accepted* or approved scholastic, *scholasticus adprobatus* – S –. This is the name given by the Jesuits to the scholastic, *scholasticus* – S –. Then he becomes priest; but he is not yet admitted to an office or posts in the *order*.

The third-degree Jesuit is the spiritual coadjutor, *coadjutor spiritualis* – C –. By a new solemn profession of the three vows of chastity, poverty and *obedience*, he is entirely incorporated into the order. He is still not admitted in the inside of the order but he is already given some posts in it.

These three kinds of Jesuits call themselves "professed of the three vows", *professi trium votorum*.

---

[83] *Mason's Hall, Mason's Alley Basinghall Street.* See the Life of Ashmole, *Biographia Britannica* [SE: *Biographia Britannica*, 7 vols. (London, 1747-63), 1, 223-36.].

[84] Idem in ibid.

[85] It is remarkable that Ramsay who knew quite well French never translated the words Free-mason when speaking about Masonry. The German people, instead of the English Free-mason, call themselves naturally Frey-maurer. It was simpler to call ourselves Franc-Maçons rather than Free-mason: a man such as Ramsey had excellent reasons for this designation.

The last or fourth Jesuit is a NOSTRE – N – Our.[86] He is the true member of the Society of Jesus, *socius societatis Jesu*, S.S.I. He takes the fourth profession: this is a vow of the most perfect obedience *to the pope*, which means clearly in their language "full of mental reservations"[87] the general of their order.

The *Our* is called a "professed of the four vows": *professus quatuor votorum*.

To become an *Our* it is necessary to have 45 years.

Based on this perfect system of four vows, the Jesuits finally changed little by little all symbols and allegories of the unique degree of the former disciples of Bacon: they made of it a Masonry that holds in servitude and ignorance close to twenty millions of men in Europe.

Let's take a preliminary look on the passwords of the lodges of Saint John – I – where everyone is a disciple of Saint Ignatius – I – without knowing it.

Masonic degrees

Apprentice	Tubalcain	T.
Fellowcraft	Schiboleth	S.
Master	Chiblim	C.
Scottish Master	Notuma	N.

Jesuitical degrees

1st Jesuit	Temporalis	T.
2d Jesuit	Scholasticus	S.
3d Jesuit	Coadjutor Spiritualis	C.
4th Jesuit	Noster	N.

All symbols of Saint John's Masons are explained by such clear numbers. The initial letters, and their numeric value in the alphabet, deserve a particular attention.

Let's recall the origin of the name FREE-MASON, Masons who were free or accepted in the guild of operative Masons. Nothing is simpler and more natural than this origin; it is easy to verify. It is even quite possible that, given

---

[86] [SE: N*oster* means *our*. The term is rarely found in contemporary English or French. The terms *Noster* and *Nostri* will be used here when the first letter N is part of a code, other wise the terms Our and Ours will be used.'

[87] [SE: *Mentalis restriction*, the doctrine of mental reservation or of mental equivocation. It was a special branch of casuistry developed in the late Middle and the Renaissance, and most often associated with the Jesuits. It is a form of deception which is not an outright lie, a way to fulfill both the obligations of telling the truth and of keeping secretes from those not entitled to know the truth.]

2. Masonry and Company of Jesus

the tendency of the time for allegories, one was very pleased to make allusion to the *House* of Salomon that will be built or Masoned.

Mr. Smith gave us two or three different opinions on the origin of this word Mason and speaks about it again a forth time in a different manner; everything that he says about the origin of this word is of an *affirmative* uncertainty that announces a mental equivocation of the highest consideration.[88]

> "I am induced to believe, said Mr. Smith, that the name of *MASON* -"

I cannot translate the word Mason in French by the word *Maçon*, without having to use other letters. According to the numbers of the alphabet, this would not give the same number, the consecrated number, anymore. This is why the Scottish Ramsay could not translate it into French.

> "... has its derivation from a *language,* in which it *implies* some strong indication, or distinction, of the nature of the society and that it has not its relationship with the architects. The French word *Maison* -"

Observe that the letter A in the English word Mason is pronounced AI as in the word *Maison* in French: Mr. Smith wanted to say the same thing while *disconcerting* the observer.

> "signifies a family or particular race of people."[89]

There are no *lost words* here: everything expresses a determined meaning. Let's analyze the word Mason according to the numeric value of the letters of the alphabet: we will recognize a *strong indication* that hides a *very specific* race of people.

In the word Mason:[90]

M	gives	12
A		1
S		18
O		14
	Total	45
	Remainder	
N		

---

[88] [SE: *The Use and Abuse of Free Masonry.* P. 17].

[89] See Footnote 85.

[90] [SE: Bonneville's deciphering suggestions seem to have been used by Agustin Barruel and Jacques Lemaire as *arguments by generalization* to reject the entirety of Bonneville's work.]

This is the initial letter of the NOSTER, of the famous *Our*, perfect degree of Jesuitism that can only be obtained after 45 years.

All the allegories are more or less of the same kind: the Jesuits have several numbers and to better veil their *mysteries* they combine them all together. Every Freemason is informed about respecting the *initial* letters of the consecrated words:[91] the anagrams, the number of points... and the set of the consonants in all syllables, etc, etc.

A small number of Masons suspect that numbers sometimes represent letters. Furthermore, a small number of them know that numbers represent letters. Without the general discovery of the system we would be strongly confused when we would know all these beautiful things: because the meaning would always remain hidden under all the mysterious abbreviations. To facilitate the laborious reading of all these combinations we believed necessary to offer an alphabetic table. The reader would only need to have a look at it to avoid the pains of a trying calculation and to verify my assertions.

ALPHABETIC TABLE.

The Letter		gives		and		gives	
	A		1		1		A
	B		2		2		B
	C		3		3		C
	D		4		4		D
	E		5		5		E
	F		6		6		F
	G		7		7		G
	H		8		8		H
	I		9		9		I
	K		10		10		K
	L		11		11		L
	M		12		12		M
	N		13		13		N
	O		14		14		O
	P		15		15		P
	Q		16		16		Q
	R		17		17		R
	S		18		18		S
	T		19		19		T
	U		20		20		U
	V		21		21		V
	X		22		22		X
	Y		23		23		Y
	Z		24		24		Z

---

[91] See Page 40 about Jackin, Boaz and Mac-Benac.

2. Masonry and Company of Jesus

The initiates, those inside the order and who know all its Jesuitical aspects, like to translate in their Latin works the French words *Maison* and *Maçon* by the Greek words LATOMOS and LATOMIA. When some Latin words are clearly used instead of these Greek words, it is almost always a sign that the writer was not Jesuit.

The Greek word *LATOMOS* means *lapicida* in Latin, *tailleur de pierre* in French, and *stonecutter* in English.
LATOMIA means *lapidicina*, the quarry, the underground, where the *stones* are found.

However, the word LATOMIA also signifies *a jail,*[92] and TOMOS a *separated* body, a body *that doesn't hold to their order.* So the Jesuits call Masons LATOMOS, to indicate men shut in lodge, their *jail*; ignorant men or *rough ashlar* that they must rough out and use with the highest skill to raise their order little by little.

Since the time when the *first* Rosicrucians of England began to assemble in the hall of the guild of Masons, the highest antiquity was hastily assigned to Masonry. As we saw, the society was incorporated to Architects and to Masons *with trowels*. The antiquarian Ashmole, one of the main members of this company of Mason workers, probably compiled everything that could have a relationship with the company of *Builders* and Architects; and gave this genealogy to the Rosicrucians, who had been accepted in the company of Masons. Ashmole is quite excusable in trying to flatter the genius of his century and his [own genius] for antiques, by all kinds of compilations, attesting the immensity of his historic knowledge to society. This genealogy was in itself *innocent* enough. His successors pushed the madness slightly further: but they had another intention; they indicated a misleading goal in the ancient times. In this way, the eye of the philosopher threw itself far away and jumped over the truth that was at his feet.

The carpet of these first Rosicrucian *Free-Masons*, before being the prey of the Jesuits, was as it is still found in a Rosicrucian book of the seventeenth century.[93]

It is a squared theater accessed by climbing seven steps. The first four steps represent the four elements, and the upper three steps represent salt, sulfur and mercury. This is the same for contemporary Rosicrucians, although gradually originating from a murky source.

---

[92] [SE: See also Bloomfield's translation of *The History of Thucydides*, 1829. Vol III. Ch. LXXXVI. P. 263, note on Latomia. See also the Ear of Dionysius in the Latomia del Paradiso, as well as A. Mackey's *Encyclopedia of Freemasonry*.]

[93] *Speculum Rhodo-Stauroticum*. [Note SE: Daniel Moegling, alias Theophilus Schweighardt. *Speculum Sophicum Rhodo Stauroticum* (*Mirror of the Wisdom of the Rosicrucians*). 1618].

In their preparatory degree, or degree of the theoretical Solomon science, the *white* apron is adorned with a ribbon that forms a square: in the days of rigorous ceremony, the lodge is illuminated with four lights.

In the second degree, or juniorat, the *white* apron has *triangular* adornments. The sign of this degree is also a *triangle*.

In the degrees that follow, no hieroglyphs are presented. However, in Germany and in Sweden, without the permission of the Superior Inconnus, chemical experiments are conducted.

After climbing the seven steps or degrees, we arrive at a squared theater that must represent all symbols of the secrets "pulled from Nature" for centuries. The two columns of Hermes are found there.[94] Each of these columns carries a sphere; they are there precisely as in the English book titled *Jachin and Boaz*.

[Figure 1 – Maier's Illustration]

The Rosicrucian meaning of the spheres is the order of creation, or the creation of nature, that was previously the object of the Mason Rosicrucians.

In the Jesuitical book *Jachin and Boaz*, there are four columns: the two front ones carry some spheres, and behind these two spherical columns we see the two other columns, which don't have a sphere.

---

[94] See *Arcana arcanissima, hoc est, Hieroglyphica Ægyptio-Græca*. [Note SE: Book from M. Maier. This illustration is from the title page. It seems to have been the first appearance of the Masonic pillars with the globes on top of the pillars.]

AUDE & TACE.

[Figure 2 – Jachin and Boaz]

This means that the ancient columns of Hermes existed before the columns of the Jesuitical temple.

In addition, the carpet shows, as that of the ancient Rosicrucians, the sun, the moon, mercury, the compass and the square.

This unique degree and this carpet of the Rosicrucians have been ported and separated in the first two degrees of Masonry. Remove from them the numbers of Jesuitism, and compare then, with the Jesuitical degrees, the goal of the first two degrees that Masonry owes to the society of the Rosicrucians. The separation is visible: there is not the slightest resemblance.

The third and fourth degrees are evidently born from political reasons having nothing common with the goal of Bacon's disciples. The difference is such that it finally led to the certainty that a demon's hand was working in the obscurity.

The passwords of the first two degrees of Masonry, *Tubalcain* and *Schibboleth* are Hebrew. The words of the last two *Mac-Benac* and *Natumad* are Gallic or ancient English. Consumed by the desire to be perceived as Templars, the word *Natumad* was mutilated later and changed into *Notuma*, to *plant* the anagram of the name d'*Aumont*, brother Templar, who, according to some, became the guardian of his order in Scotland.

It is unlikely that Gallic was spoken at the time of Salomon; but the Superior Inconnus didn't expect that the best scholars of a century would meet to study their symbols. The passwords of the Rosicrucians were *tacendo* and *sperando*, T. S. which meant for the initiates: In silence we hope.

The words *Jachin* and *Boaz*, I. B. are only of yesterday: the word *Chiblim*, given at the Master Degree, is the word *Giblim* of the Holly Scripture. Instead of the G, pronounced K, the CH, also pronounced K in Latin, was adopted. But the major reason of this change is that the initial letter needed to be a C. The allusion to their spiritual coadjutor needed to be more obvious: C, or third Jesuitical degree.

Without a Jesuitical motive, it would be impossible to find a pretext to the awful formula of the oath that the initiates must take.

In the old Rosicrucian meetings, *things* were said; the virtue of the minerals and plants was covered. There it was about poisons causing miraculous cures when used cautiously. Finally since the medical art could only be confided to discreet men, a solemn promise was perceived as necessary. Now in most lodges of our Freemasons, where allegories *that are printed everywhere* are only *figured*, it is a horror to require a loathsome oath for this sometimes terrifying initiation!

What an atrocity it is to make thousands of men pay considerable taxes, in the hope to learn a secret that they must never have!

Mr. Smith, who is however English, says that it is very rare that the *Masonic secret* is confided to Englishmen.[95] Does this country of liberty ever lack great men!

The real reason of the silence of the Superior Inconnus towards Englishmen is their ban of the Scottish dagger; it is their eternal enmity against the Jesuits driven away by them.

When considering that the unfortunate Charles I, king of England, had a taste for chemical studies, we can conclude some that he was not least eager to encourage the efforts of his Rosicrucian Masons. The astrologer Lilly, a Rosicrucian *accepted* like the others in the company of the body of Masons with *trowels*, was a favorite of Charles I.

It is therefore natural to think that as soon as some armed fanatics made the king tremble every day, the entire Society of the Rosicrucian Masons formed a league with him against the fanatics and the parliament. The antiquarian Ashmole, Rosicrucian Mason, lost one of his lands as he stood for the unfortunate Charles his protector. Another member of the society, George Wharton, sold all his goods and raised some troops for the king's party. All these circumstances, attested by history, are sufficient enough to convince us that the Rosicrucian Masons consulted one another, in their assemblies, on the king's business.

Charles I was beheaded. Because of Cromwell's politics, it was dangerous for the king's partisans to be discovered. The heirs of the kingdom were admitted in the society of Rosicrucian Masons who were suspected to be the partisans of the royal family. Under the pretext of a political goal, secret assemblies were held in the interest of the royal family: New signs and symbols were chosen to ascertain the reciprocal confidence during one's journeys, either in the provinces of England or in Holland, where the Royal Family was.

---

[95] *The Use and abuse of Free Masonry.* On masonic hieroglyphs. Page 166.

2. Masonry and Company of Jesus

They painted *their master* killed; it was Charles I. They looked for *the lost word*, which is the *royal word* of Charles' son who they wanted to put back on throne. They called the king's son the *widow's child*, because the queen was then the head of the family. They changed the signs of the Rosicrucian Masons for greater safety.

In the chaos of the anarchy that followed the death of Cromwell and the expulsion of his son Richard, patriots wished the recall of the son of Charles I to save the damaged homeland: but they had little hope to get this recall. While generals of the English armies were not always agreeing among themselves, they agreed however to proscribe all idea favorable to the royal family.

General Monk who commanded an English army in Scotland was the only one of all generals who secretly wished the restoration of the royal dignity.

The secret society of the king's friends based all its expectations on the Scottish army: Suddenly they suspected some members of disloyalty; and they made between themselves an even sterner choice to maintain their immediate relationships with the army of Scotland. They chose some symbols conforming to their critical state. General Monk and the Rosicrucian Masons succeeded. Charles II was enthroned.

The secret history of the restoration of Charles II to the throne[96] clearly shows that a number of Jesuits took advantage of the results of the civil war to gain entry into the society of the Rosicrucian Masons.

Besides the clarifications from this secret history, we must note that the animals dedicated to the emblems that suddenly appeared on the carpet of the degraded Rosicrucians, are all Jesuitical animals: it is not simply because they figure today on the carpet of the Scottish Masters: it is because they are drawn from the emblems of their very honored brother *Typotius*.[97]

When General Monk triumphed over the enemies of Charles II, the symbols of the Rosicrucian Masons who expressed their relationships with the Scottish army became useless: they abandoned them.

Under Charles II the customs and the sciences underwent a major revolution. The political business of the Rosicrucian Masons stopped at his restoration. In addition, the most essential members of the society foresaw fatal consequences in their relationships with worried and ambitious members who moved away entirely from their primary ideas, and *left the society*.

This is when the Jesuits began to carve in full material. Then, by turns with some insolence and suppleness, they were able to revive the terrifying *Scottish symbols* for their purpose.

---

[96] See *The secret history of White-Hall, from the restoration of Charles II down to the abdication of the late K. James*, by D. Jones London 1697.

[97] *Typotii emblemata* 1601. [SE: This is the *Symbola divina et humana* by Jacobus Typotius, a Flemish humanist who became court historian to the Emperor Rudolph II. This work in three volumes was an influential collection of emblems and imprese. The engravings were by Aegidius Sadeler. See also Yarker's *The Arcane Schools*. 2006. P. 448.]

The history of Freemasonry as found in the calendars of the Masons of Saint John indicates the times, precisely and yet allegorically.
The allegorical history of this calendar mentions that SAINT ALBAN introduced Masonry in England and that he opened a first lodge.

SAINT ALBAN is Charles I.

Next it mentions that this first lodge of SAINT ALBAN existed until the reign of Athelstan who, at the solicitation of his brother Edwin, granted the *Freemasons* a *Free Charter*.

N.B. History specifies that Athelstan did not have a brother Edwin but two brothers, Edmonds and Edred.[98] The calendar of the Masons of Saint John is therefore as impudently false as is the secret history of the inner sanctuary. To speak *pertinently*, this history is only an allegory: and it is easy enough to untangle.
S. Alban is the unfortunate Charles, first by name and first martyr of the royalty in England.
Athelstan is Charles II, his son, who, upon the solicitation of his brother the Duke of York, granted the Jesuits distinguished favors.
This brother of Charles II, who succeeded him next under the name of Jacques II, founded publicly in London a college of Jesuits. This college is called naturally in the history of Jesuitized Freemasons, the Grand Lodge of York, because Jacques II established his college of Jesuits when he was still Duke of York.
How could this king S. Alban have opened a Grand Lodge of catholic Freemasons in England in 287, since then he was– what is called a *pagan*!
The reign of Athelstan started in 925. Who could suspect some mystery to the number 926 to which is attributed a great masonic event?
But why putting on the throne the ghost of a king who was never established. In 1358, the generous Edwin could not have revised the Masonic constitution; as king of England, since Edward III reigned in 1358.[99] And this Edward III then bothered by a violent war, had too many personal concerns to think about a masonic revision.
Therefore these assertions are evidently false: let us prove the allegorical intention, and carry the torch of analysis up into the treasure of *the mental reservations*.
The first establishment of Masonry occurred under Charles I in 1646. There is a fact.
According to the calendar, S. Alban established a first lodge in 287. There is an allegory.
At first glance, we cannot really figure out the resemblance between

---

[98] Davis Hume. *The History of England*. Vol. I.
[99] See Hume *in ibid*.

2. Masonry and Company of Jesus

1646 and 287.

While these dates appear so different, let us sum them up and look at the results:

```
1
6           2
4  1646     8   287
6           7
___         ___
17          17
```

The sum of the numbers marking the year of the Masonic establishment in 287 is 17. There is *some appearance* of allusion to the real time of this establishment which was in 1646 under Charles I where the sum of the numbers also gives 17.

It was in 1682 that the Jesuits made of the House of Salomon of Bacon a Salomon's *temple*: a house can hardly be but a house or laboratory, while homage or genuflexions can easily be demanded under the arch of a *temple*: there, altars can be raised and god-like venerations practiced. Is it not precisely about the Jesuits that the Holy Scriptures write: *You will be like gods*. I am not joking: open Pascal anywhere.

> Hoping to provide a first outline of the morals of the Jesuits, Pascal wrote, "I am only copying their own words. "They are a society of men, or rather let us call them angels, *predicted by Isaiah* in these words, '*Go, ye swift and ready angels*.'"[100]

Let us sum up the numbers representing the true date of the introduction of the Jesuits in the laboratory of the Rosicrucian Masons, and the establishment of their college in London by the Duke of York, brother of Charles II.

Let us see if the numbers 9, 2 and 6 of the reign of Athelstan, who could not have been solicited to protect the Jesuits by a brother he didn't have, will provide us the sum of the numbers that compose the year 1682, when Charles II, who had a brother, allowed him, as Duke of York, to create a first college of Jesuits in London:

```
            1
9           6
2  926      8   1682
6           2
___         ___
17          17
```

---

[100] *Imago Primi Saeculi* and Pascal, [*The Provincial letters*], Letter V.

No matter how boring all these calculations are, it is necessary to pay an analytic attention here: they give this Jesuitical part *an air of grimoire* that represents quite well their charlatanism.

These swift and ready angels were chased away from England in 1718. This is when they established the *high degrees* of Scottish Masonry: the purpose of these high degrees was the construction of a *second* temple, the temple of Esdras.

Ready minds, tell us *swiftly*, why did want to build a *second temple*, if the first one *was still standing*? If even, according to Mr. Smith, it did not endure any outrage from the forge of time from the good Adam until your Superior *Inconnus*?

I know you are *swift* to build, but *very slow* to answer. One would solicit you for a long time in vain. Therefore, I will begin to speak, and avoid the details that don't smell enough like the *Sovereign of Sovereigns* to be permitted to you.

By *order* of the Jesuits, or on behalf of the *king of kings*, their general, a Masonry was created with the purpose of building a temple for them. This Masonry had to be useful to their benefactor Jacques II or to the Pretender.

Jesuit-like catechism or Masonic meeting

"Why was Jacques II called Edwin, who was never king of England?
It is evidently to indicate an allegorical history.

"Why was Jacques II called Edwin and the Pretender Edwin as well?"
It is because it is of common usage that the son carries his father's name.

"In what year was this construction of the second temple of Esdras prepared?"
In 1358 under the reign of Edwin.

"But how is it that king Edward reigned then? He had too many enemies to worry about to take care of the capricious reconstruction of a temple. I say capricious, because since the first temple was standing straight and strong, the second one was not indispensable."
It is because in 1718 the English dared chasing out the MASONS (and in a very low voice, the *Jesuits*); they will pay us dearly this impertinence!

"Assure yourselves of the sum of the numbers of the allegorical year 1358 and of the real year 1718, when the English chassed out the *Lower* masons (and in a very low voice, the *Jesuits*)."

I have summed up, Most Respectable: they give an equal number:

2. Masonry and Company of Jesus

1		1	
3	1358	7	1718
5		1	
8		8	
17		17	

Did you observe that both the historic and symbolic years give have the number 17 as the result of the sum? Explain this phenomenon to me."
My Respectable, in the historic years all is in conformity with the annals of our Europe: it is therefore an effect of *luck*: but in the other case all facts are altered; therefore these numbers 17 are about an allegory, even more so ingenious, that all assertions that it gives us are free.

"You answer too well, *dear brother*, for us not to confess onto you what the great number of OUR VERY-WORTHY ELECTS certainly doesn't know.
"The situation is identical for these fables found in our historic almanac about Queen Elizabeth.
"If the almanac, that sells rather expensively, means nothing, so much the better; so much the better for Masons: it could teach them *how to live*."

How, Most Venerable, would it not be true that Queen Elisabeth persecuted Masons with an atrocious cruelty? And that she destroyed the Grand Lodge in December 1561? Who is the scoundrel who dared giving us such a history, to me especially whose time is so precious for the secret matters of my mission? *It is therefore a lie: why did you write it? Si falsa, cur scripsit* [If false, why did you write it], said energetically St Jerome in his thirty-sixth Epistle: My century has been highly slandered, Most Venerable; I think today as one thought in the time of Homer, when one had a heart.

Achilles answered, "… Him do I hate even as the gates of hell who says one thing while he hides another in his heart".[101]

"Very dear brother, I am *delighted* to see that you have a sensitive heart and a local memory,[102] and one can only learn with such an enlightened brother. Now, we must close the lodge, very dear brethren; to me, my brethren; *let's tyle*, my brethren."

---

[101] Homer. *The Iliad*, [Book IX,] verse 312.
[102] [SE: Local memory: system in which one associates commonplaces with symbols. Expression used by Racine in his notes on memory. See *Fragmentary voices: memory and education at Port-Royal*, by Nicholas Hammond. 2004]

Other meeting of the Jesuit fathers

Here is an immature little scattered-brained person: We acted quite wisely by expelling him politely from the sanctuary: I know you more discreet, and I want to instruct you a little bit.

"Everything that our calendar says about Elizabeth and about her bad mood is a delicious allegory of all that happened at that time in France."

Indeed I remember that the historian De Thou, a Frenchman, in his thirty-fifth book, page 735, mentions all the Statutes that the French clergy, assembled in Poissy in 1561, bear against the Jesuits.[103]

"It is precisely the time of 1561, dedicated allegorically to Elizabeth's reign.

The whole France was indignant against the college of Clermont: At the time, the Sorbonne was not standing by us. The college of Clermont, in the code of our Masonic calendars, is nothing else but the entire Society of the Jesuits. The establishment of the Jesuits in England is the Grand Lodge of York, which represents our former college of Clermont in Paris. So when we wrote that in 1561 the Grand Lodge of York had been persecuted, it seems that we expressed through a rather clear allegory the Statutes of the French clergy assembled in Poissy against the college of Clermont.

Here it is, very dear brother, the useful use of our admirable doctrine of equivoques, by which 'it is permitted to use ambiguous terms, leading people to understand them in another sense from that in which we understand them ourselves.'"[104]

Pious and holy finesse! *Piam et religiosam calliditatem*, as it is written in "The Image of the First Century."[105]

"In the famous list of the great events of Masonry, page 34, I find that the architect *Inigo Jones* constituted various lodges in England."

Was it not in 1607 that the society of Don *Inigo de Guiposcoa* was very active in England? Is it necessary to remind you that this Don Inigo de

---

[103] [SE: Jacques Auguste de Thou (Thuanus) (1553-1617). French historian, book collector and president of the Parlement de Paris. His main work, the *Historia sui temporis*, comprised originally 138 books in Latin. They were later translated several times, including the *Histoire universelle*, Fr. trans. by C. le Beau, Le Mascrier, the Abbé Des Fontaines (16 volumes) in 1734.]

[104] Thomas Sanchez. op. mor. p. 2, l. 3. chap6. N° 13, cited in Blaise Pascal. *The Provincial Letters*, letter IX.

[105] [SE: Blaise Pascal. The Provincial Letters, letter X, referring to the *Imago Primi Saeculi* (Image of the First Century), Book II Or. I and Book I, c. II.]

2. Masonry and Company of Jesus

Guiposcoa later called himself *Ignatius of Loyola*. He was a valiant knight and Voltaire, who wrote history like a vagrant, presented him as the *least political* mind of the world.[106] However we call him, under the pretext of a good word of the Grand Condé, [107] another Caesar.

> "Voltaire may try to turn our great saint in ridicule, represented ascending to heaven in a coach with four white horses;[108] we will see him again on our altars, this great architect of the holy temple. What I find at least as pleasing and a lot more cheerful, it is that Voltaire was himself one of our domestic servants: he didn't suspect it, the poor man! You can say that this is quite an achievement. Did you read the book on *Adonhiramite* Masonry? Voltaire's views were quite exposed in it!"

Would it be one of our last French publications, small booklet in appearance that doesn't say anything!

> "One should not stay at the level of the bark."

Per Saint Ignatius, the lucky book is sold at the former Jesuit Church.[109]

> "By chance. It is there that fortunately luck gathered our sheep-like Masonry; beautiful ashlar to rough-hew, money, always money, and sometimes gold. "

Very dear brother ... A discovery! My God! A word no more than that. – You drag me into the thorns. Would it not be there? ... Answer, answer please, very dear brother!

> "Maybe!"

Could this be possible? Would this be ... some golden palms? The inconnu [unknown] *Magnum Opus*?

"Inconnu [Unknown] - I."
Jesuitic?

---

[106] Voltaire. *Essai sur les mœurs et l'esprit des nations* [*Essay on the Manner and Spirit of Nations*], chap. 139.

[107] [SE: Louis de Bourbon, Prince of Condé (1621 –1686) was a French general and the most famous representative of the Condé branch of the House of Bourbon. Prior to his father's death in 1646, he was styled the Duc d'Enghien. For his military prowess he was renowned as le *Grand Condé*.]

[108] Voltaire. *Essai sur les mœurs et l'esprit des nations*. Vol. 8

[109] [SE: Église des Jésuites, nowadays the parish church Sainte-Trinité-et-Saint-Georges.]

".... It is you who named it!"

<hr>

In 1607 the Society of the Jesuits was very active in England: one of these good fathers was quartered there because of his excessive activity.[110] To write in their annals this time of a great distress in the Masonic constitutions, they first placed their *grand architect* Inigo *allegorically* instead of the society; and to throw another veil on their Jesuitical number, they chose architect *Inigo Jones* to represent their terrifying Inigo de Guiposcoa, who is hardly known but under the name of Ignatius of Loyola, name dedicated to secret worships.

The Masonic Fables of the Superior Inconnus mention that the protector Cromwell had found in White-hall some papers that he did not understand. This is again an allusion to the great danger faced by the Society of Jesus when a copy of their constitutions seized from one of their OURS was published in England: but they escaped the danger and the secret papers could not be read then.

"Would we always have eyes to not see?"

To evaluate the politics, the villainy and the genius of Cromwell, it is sufficient to know that he used the Jesuits to oppress his rivals, and then he overwhelmed them with all his power. This is why, in the book titled *Ancient and New Mysteries*, Cromwell is called a great antagonist of the order.[111]

We still find today at the Magdalen College in Oxford, former college of the Jesuits, quantity of allegorical monuments and hieroglyphs that can shed a light on the symbols of the Masons of Saint John.[112]

Irrevocable proof of the relationship between *Jesuitism* and Masonry. St John's College is the only one of all colleges of Jesuits whose residence is not marked on the public list of their colleges.

Why St John's College has no set location, while the other colleges do?

St John's College, *without residence* on the list of the colleges of the Jesuits, allegorically means *the lodge of Saint* John.

In Masonic style *the lodge of Saint John* expresses the first three degrees of the *royal art*.

<hr>

[110] Jubileum S. Speculum Jesuiticum, 1643, page 120.

[111] Alte und neue Mysterien [Johan Starck. Berlin. 1782], pag. 276.

[112] See *Mémoires de la dernière révolution d'Angleterre*, by Mr. L. B. T. *In The Hague, 1702, in-8°* [Guillaume de Lamberty. Memorial of the last England revolution containing the abdication of Jacques II, the advent of his majesty king Guillaume III to the crown and several other things arrived under his reign. The Hague, 1702.].

2. Masonry and Company of Jesus

St John's College is located among the other colleges of the Jesuits, to express that Masonry is *between the hands* of the Jesuits.

The residence of *St John*'s College could not be determined because *the lodge of Saint John* expresses allegorically the assemblies of the perfect Masons, who are everywhere in Europe, and who already begin to spread to the other regions of the world.

The first Rosicrucian Masons only had one carpet: the Jesuits made two degrees of this same carpet to adapt Masonry to the professions of the *temporal* and the *scholastic*, their novices.

The carpet of the Rosicrucian Masons was a *perfect* square. The Jesuits transformed it into an oblong square so that this carpet was the perfect emblem of a temple.[113]

The oblong square, symbol of a temple, was always the favorite emblem of the Jesuits.

The last book of François Riberas on the temple of Jerusalem speaks about its width and its length; about everything that was found in the *Holy Temple*, or *Templum Societatis*, or *Temple of Jerusalem*, *Templum Jesuitarum*. All these measures and distributions were seen in the past on the *oblong* carpet of the Scottish of Saint Andrew.[114].

The reception of the Jesuits and of all religious people in general occurs in front of the altar with the forehead facing the east. The reception of our Jesuit Masons brethren is identical.

The rituals and *catechisms* of the numerous systems of Freemasonry, in spite of their *obvious* difference, also have the four major points of meeting that indicate a same source and a same purpose.

As soon as the Jesuits appropriated the society of the Rosicrucian Masons, they made a sacerdotal *order* of it. The whole society imperceptibly conformed to their *celibate* institution: the allegories, the symbols and the interpretations prepare a *hierarchy* of *celibate* priests whose intention is to govern the whole world there from afar.

The contemporary carpet of Jesuit Freemasons still carries the Rosicrucian hieroglyphs.

---

[113] *Masonry dissected.* - Rabani Mauri opera Col. Agr. sol. Tom II. and Franc. Riberae lib. of Templ. Hierosolymitano, *Salamanca*. 1623 [SE: ?? Francisco de Ribera (1537-1591) of Salamanca Spain. De Templo Hierosolymitano et iis, quae ad templum pertinent, libri V, *Salamant.*].

[114] This is validated by comparing the description of the temple of Jerusalem by the Jesuit Riberas and the description of the carpet of the Scottish of Saint Andrew [écossais de Saint-André], in one German book that has for title, *Allerneuste Entdeckungen der F.M.* 1781 [SE: Probably *Allerneuste Entdeckung der verborgensten Geheimisse der hohen Stuffen der Freimaurerei* (1766: *Les Plus Secrets Mystères des Hauts Grades de la Maçonnerie Dévoilés* [The Most Secret Mysteries of the High Grades of Masonry Unveiled. See translation by Eric Serejski, 32° and S. Brent Morris, 33°].]

The two columns of Hermes: However the Gnostic spheres now have disappeared from these two ancient columns. An I and a B are carved on them.

We also see there the seven rungs, a cabalistic number.

They also have the squared floor, the square, the sun, and the moon.

The Blazing Star of our Jesuit Masons comes from the carpet of the Rosicrucian Masons, but the one of the first Rosicrucians had five blazing points: it was visibly the star pentagon of the Seven Sages of Greece. The Blazing Star of the Jesuit Masons has six angles, and some times even seven. It is necessary to observe that a G is soiling the Pythagorean pentagon.

A *rough ashlar* and a *perfect ashlar* have been added on the *oblong* carpet. When precisely drawn, this ashlar figures a square *below* and a triangle *above*.

The level shaped in a triangle is a modern and Jesuitical invention.

They had some windows in the east, west and south. They are not seen anymore on their carpet, or rarely.

The indented tessel, [115] a true belt of monk, is a ministerial allegory, as one can imagine.

The explanations given in lodge to the poor Masons are so *obvious*, that they are printed in all languages. The catechisms state that the real meaning must be guessed: the Freemasons must never learn them from another Mason. [116] This is how they must always be dependent from the Superior Inconnus – S. I. – *Societas Jesuitarum*.

We are going to give the real explanation of all the symbols stained by the Jesuits in the allegories of the Bacon's disciples.

.... Deus haec fortasse benigna. Reducet in sedem vice ...

Perhaps Providence by some happy changes will restore those things to their proper places? [117]

The lodge of Saint John represents Salomon's temple, that is to say, the temple of the Society of the Jesuits. It is the temple of a universal hierarchy. The titles *Right Reverend* and *Worshipful* represent rather well the ecclesiastical state of the Freemasons.

The *two columns* always mean the church in the language of theologians.

The full explanation about the mysterious letters I and B, or as written previously B and I, requires to say first that the seven rungs are explained here by the seven ordinations of priesthood, which are indispensable to enter in the order of the Jesuits.

---

[115] [SE: houppe dentelée, indented tassel, known under the corrupted term indented tarsel.]

[116] See *Masonry Dissected*.

[117] Horace. Epodes, Carmen. XIII 7-8 [Also translated as "God perchance will by a happy change restore these things to a settled condition".]

2. Masonry and Company of Jesus

The oblong floor is here the square of the temple or novitiate of the order.

The square means the *obedience* and full submission to the rule of the Jesuitical order.

The compass is only for the Masters.

The sun is the order of the Jesuits.[118]

The ornament of the Grand Elect Knights is a sun *with nine rays*. This expresses the nine suns or founders of the Order of the Jesuits.

When someone establishes himself as *god* once, it is easy for him to establish himself as *a sun*. Too much modesty is not the shortcoming of the humble Jesuits.

The moon is the order of the Freemasons: this moon draws its light from the sun, that is to say, from the Society of the Jesuits.

The Rosicrucian Masons had naturally taken the moon as one of their recognition signs. The tavern, where the antiquarian Ashmole and the Rosicrucian Masons attended Masonic banquets, had a *crescent* moon for sign.[119]

The moon is always represented by the Jesuits *half*-illuminated; in other words, it is only illuminated on *one* side. Mr. Starcke, in his treatise *on the Mysteries*,[120] had the moon engraved *all alone* on the frontispiece of his book. Why this moon all alone? The allegory is perfect: the order of the Jesuits doesn't shine anymore *on the horizon*. The Jesuitical sun must be hidden.

It is for this *temporary* eclipse of the Jesuitical sun, that the famous *Noachite* degree – N –, *the highest degree* among the high degrees of their Scottish Masonry, is only held in the full moon. The lodge is then only illuminated by a window through which the moon rays beam. Imagine in the silence of the night the pale rays of the moon that illuminate men armed with daggers. Then avoid, if you can, thinking about a conjuration of brigands!

The G in the *Blazing Star* means the *General* of the Jesuits. The rays of the star represent the *assistants* chosen by the General among his *Ours*.

This symbolic G is explained allegorically in the famous book of Samuel Prichard, an ancient catechism that the new Jesuits believed forgotten. The Jesuit Prichard states in his catechism that the G symbolizes "the Grand Architect and Contriver of the Universe, or HE *that was taken up to the Top of the Pinnacle of the Holy Temple.*"[121]

---

[118] See *Imago Primi Saeculi*, Fol. Antwerp. 1641. [SE: The "Image of the First Century of the Society of Jesus" or *Imago primi Saeculi Societatis Iesu a Provincia Flandro-Belgico eiusdem Societatis representata*. Antwerp. 1640.]

[119] Biographia Britannica, Volume I, page 743.

[120] [Abhandlung über die Geheimnisse. [SE: This is probably Johann August von Starck (1741-1816), a prolific author and Freemason. For study on Starck, see Telepneff, 1928, and Alain Bernheim 33°, *Johann August Starck (Schwerin 1741 - Darmstadt 1816). The Templar Legend and the Clerics.*

[121] See *Masonry Dissected*. P. 164.

These primitive names of "Grand Architect and Contriver of the Universe" are only translated nowadays as *Grand Architect of the Universe*. However in the Jesuitical writings the Universe means the Jesuitical order, the hierarchy of the Jesuits. Additionally, *order and Universe* are almost always synonymous for the Jesuits; one says *order* for *Universe* because order must govern the Universe. Finally one says *universe* for *order* because the whole world or the universe swarms with Masons dedicated to Saint John; and that these innumerable Masons are slaves chained by the Jesuits, *rough ashlars* that the Jesuits would like to hew. To express *the assembly of all their lodges*, why wouldn't they say allegorically the *Universe*? We do say in Paris *l'université, universitas*, to express the meeting of all our Parisian colleges.

In the *Rosicrucian* degree of the Knight of the Sword, the CHAIR Master is expressly called the General of *Jerubabel* – I – because in the degree all Rosicrucian brethren are called *Jerubabel – I –*.

The General of the Jerubabels – I – is *evidently* the General of the *Jesuits*. – I –.

It was *Zorobabel* who rebuilt the temple of Esdras: it was not Jerubabel. However, the initial letter I was needed: an alteration resembling the one for their *Chiblim* was made with Zorobabel. To disfigure the Holy Scripture is of no cost to them!

There are no modern languages where Z is pronounced like I; there are no texts in the Holy Scriptures where the name Zorobabel is altered. In the *table of contents* of the Vulgate, the editor wrote *Sorobabel* and *Zorobabel*. [His purpose was] to facilitate research; because in nearly all languages the S is often pronounced like a Z. However *in the text* it is always *Zorobabel*: this holds true for the Greek Bible published by Sixtus V and Clement VIII, for the Vulgate of Saint Jerome and for the French translation of Lemaistre de Sacy. Nothing allows this modification except a *premeditated intention*: in the Greek, Latin and French, it is always Zorobabel who built the temple of Esdras.[122]

This observation is important: It is without retort, and Pyrrho himself would have found difficult to escape this *ad hominem* argument! It is even an *ad angelos* argument, and I believe that the most cautious option for our *swift an ready angels* is to fly off at night taking advantage of the silence of a *friendly moon: Per amica silentia lunae*.[123]

The same catechism of Samuel Prichard, says again while speaking of the – G –: "But none but Males shall know my Mind." And he adds: "By Letters Four and *Science Five*, This G aright doth *stand*."[124]

---

[122] 2 Esdras 12:1 [SE: This should be Esdras 3:2], Matthew 1:13, Luke 3:27 and Ecclesiastes Si 49:13 [SE: This should be Si 49:11]. [SE: Zorobabel is the Greek term ζοροβαβελ for the Hebrew Zrubavel זְרֻבָּ־בֶל. The traditional English term is Zerubbabel. The Greek term appears 24 times in the Bible.]

[123] [SE: Virgil, *The Aeneid*, BkII:255]

[124] See *Masonry Dissected*. P. 165.

2. Masonry and Company of Jesus

These four letters that one must know are printed as follows: G.A.I.N. in the Jesuitical book titled *The [Most] Secret Mysteries of the High Grades of Masonry Unveiled*.

These letters signify GENERALIS – G – the General, ASSISTENTES – A – the Assistants, Jesuitae – J – the Jesuits, NOSTRI – N – Ours.

G.A.I.N. being explained, the science of the *five* is not very difficult to grasp: the five points of Mastery are simply the five duties of a Jesuit *Our* as a General! Zeal, vigilance, hardihood, courage and constancy are the five duties of a general of the Jesuits required by their founder Don Inigo of Guiposcoa.[125]

In the lodges the G is explained by the word GOD, because the General of the Order of the Jesuits, according to a famous historian, is God's REPRESENTATIVE.[126]

The G in the Blazing Star can only symbolize the General of the Order. One must confess that a god *standing up* on *his feet* looks strongly like a man: it can only be rigorously a man, and allegorically The KING OF KINGS, an ALMIGHTY MAN, a God-MAN, a GOD'S REPRESENTATIVE. Therefore it is the General of the Jesuits, since the general of the Jesuits is called, par excellence, *God's Representative*; The one who *holds God's place, locum Dei tenens*.[127]

The Blazing Star with six rays of today's Rosicrucians includes an eye. This eye is explained in the book *Jachin and Boaz* as "the Eye of *Providence* or the *Great Superintendant* of all the works of the *Universe*".

Providence – P – the Great Superintendant – G – S – that is to say, *Praepositus* P *generalis societatis* – G – S – General of the society.[128]

Some carpets have no G in the Blazing Star: but they figure seven small stars: this always comes back to the same because the letter G is the seventh letter of the alphabet.

There are researchers of the philosophical stone who say that the G of the Blazing Star is the initial of the English and German words that means gold, *gold* in English and *golt* in German. For those people, the seven Stars enclosed in the Blazing Star are the seven planets of the crucible!

---

[125] See *Histoire [de l'admirable] dom Inigo de Guiposcoa*. The Hague 1723. P. 180 [SE: *History (the) of the wonderful Don Ignatius de Loyola, founder of the Order of the Jesuits; with an account of the establishment and government of that Order*. Translated from the French [of Hercule Rasiel de Selva, *i.e.* Pasquier Quesnel, or Charles Gabriel Porée]. 12mo. 2 vols. [*Brit. Mus.*] London, 1754].

[126] Generalis jesuitarum est locum Dei tenens. See Harenberg's Geschichte der Jesuiten, Vol 1, p. 78. [SE: J.C. Harenberg, *Pragmatische Geschichte des Ordens der Jesuiten* (Halle-Helmstadt: Hemmerle, 1760), 2 Volumes]

[127] [SE: For a discussion on the Jesuit concept of one's superior being God, See *The Church of England Quarterly Review*. XVIII. 1845. P. 318.]

[128] See Masonry Dissected.

May the God of Israel and of Jacob hold them in his very holy and worthy guard!

"Poor people, how I pity them! For one always entertains, for fools, more of pity than of anger." [(La Fontaine. Fable VII, 12)]

In the alleged Egyptian lodges, this G is mysteriously explained as *Jehovah* – I –. Therefore, this cannot *masonically* be the initial for golt or gold, consequently it is not gold bar: it is *simply pure* Jesuitism. Most of these Egyptian Masons do not know that the initial of Jehovah is an I and not a G.

The anonymous author of the book on *Adonhiramite* Masonry was much embarrassed to insert the *truth* in the catechism, and however to hide it from the Masons to whom this crafty *catechism* seems intended: a note was inserted; and with the help of this well prepared note, the number 7 symbolizes the famous G, *the seventh letter of the alphabet*.

It also includes the name of the builder of the second temple, carefully called *Jerubabel*.

Representing simultaneously Ignatius and Jesuit, their famous column became dearest to them.

According to the catechism of Samuel Prichard, at first one always saw Boaz before Jachin, that is to say, B. before I. on the carpet of apprentices. This expressed faithfully *Beatus Ignatius*, B.I.

It must be very rare in France to find the B. before the I.; because the Jesuits soon perceived that the allegory was slightly too clear, and they changed the numbers of their columns. However in a small book titled "Règlements pour la loge des Neuf-Sœurs à l'Orient de Paris, l'an de la vénérable loge 5779" [Regulations of the Lodge of the Nine Sisters at the Orient of Paris, year of the Worshipful Lodge 5779], I find on the Frontispiece B. before I. I also find there a dagger submitted to a crown. Finally I recognize the Jesuitical hand there: but after having browsed through the names of the members composing this lodge, and finding there mostly the elite of Men of Letters, I can hardly suspect that they participated knowingly in this dishonoring frontispiece. Voltaire, one of the members of this lodge, was far from lending a sacrilegious hand to the establishment of a hierarchy of monks. These Jesuits always expose the great Voltaire in the list of the Freemasons their slaves. However they do not ignore that Voltaire wrote, in his *Questions about the Encyclopedia*, that the *mysteries of the poor Freemasons were rather dull*: but Voltaire's name is known more than his writings; his name is sufficient to bring them the multitude. His writings having moved away their symbol from the *eye of literate people*, they had a free field in France. Without the anonymous book *Adonhiramite Masonry* and some others, I could never have believed that Masonry in France was not a game: it is the importance that one attaches to it in foreign countries, and the research provided to me, that rendered me attentive.

Emperor Joseph II probably doesn't think like Voltaire that the mysteries of the poor Freemasons are rather dull: he knows, as a clever politician, that it

2. Masonry and Company of Jesus

is not necessary to neglect the mysterious purpose of the leaders of a numerous society. All his stern regulations against the order and his considerations for every isolated member prove his concerns or at least his suspicions. It is up to the reader's to judge if they are founded.

The lodge of *Beatus Ignatius* is situated in the Valley of Josaphat, I: again the Jesuits, I.

The Superior Inconnus, or Unknown Philosophers, want to express a same thing: *Superiores Incogniti*, S.I. that is to say, *Societas Iesu*, S.I.

The *rough* ashlar is the profane world or the first degree of the Jesuits; because it is only in the second degree that one begins to enter in their order. In the second degree the *perfect* ashlar is provided.

The base of this ashlar is a *square*, because the order is based on the *Ours*, that is, on the Jesuits who professed the *four vows*. This is why in the Scottish degree one knocks four times four. In the first three degrees one only hits by three, because one is there again *professed* of three vows only.

The plumb shaped as a triangle signifies perfect *obedience, omne trinum perfectum* [everything in threes is perfect].

The ornament of the NOACHITE is *a triangle with an arrow* whose tip is turned downward. In the symbolic language of the Jesuits, "*the vows of the order are expressed by arrows*";[129] these are *strokes* that go to the heart.

There are no windows in the north: no *light* in the north. When the Jesuits disfigured the carpet of the Rosicrucian Masons, they put three windows on their new carpet; a window in the east, another in the west and another in the south! But why they didn't put any light in the north? It is because the *celibate* priests were despised there; it is because there were no Jesuits there. Therefore all *was darkness there*.

The Jesuits could have said that in 1682! Today some say that the sun *begins to penetrate in the north*: it is because today, as we know, some Jesuits are found in Russia, in Sweden and in Denmark.

The indented tassel is the sign of the perfect *reunion* of a harmonious operation: it is an emblem stolen from Christianity by the Jesuits. The Jesuits seek to obtain this *unity*, this *harmonious* will, by an absolute obedience to the General's orders.

In the Masonic analysis by Samuel Prichard, the tassel is called indented, jagged: but *indenture*, in English, means a convention, an alliance, a contract. In the order of the Mopses the tassel is spread around the whole carpet. The book titled *Les secrets des Mopses*[130] states on page 166 that "All members must be Romans Catholics." Therefore, it is not a *pagan* who instituted

---

[129] See *Imago primi saeculi*, p. 16

[130] [SE: This is actually *L'ordre des francs maçons trahi et Le secret des Mopses*, 1745, by GLC Pérau. This pleasant exposure constitutes from some JD Hamilton and P Négrier a documentary on Freemasonry at the time of its introduction in France in the beginning of the 18th century.]

Freemasonry in England: but let's speak about what Jesuits understand by catholicity.[131]

The *universality* of the religion of the Jesuits, is nothing else than the *university* of their colleges, their assemblies, their jails or lodges; these words are all allegorically synonymous. Besides [the entirety of the works of] Pascal show how the Jesuits are far from preaching *Christendom*; this holy religion whose first precept *is to love one's brother*.

Far from ordering *vengeance* like the *Jesuits* do, the *Messenger of God* orders to make peace with one's brother before daring to raise one's heart toward the throne where he sits in Heaven!

The Jesuitical *catholicity* is the universal monarchy that they hope to get one day by a first institution of celibates.

Let's pass to the ceremonies of the reception. The striping of his clothes up to the belt and of all his metals is used by the Jesuits and in all orders of celibates where a novice is received *monk*.

This word must be explained; one doesn't suspect what it means for the Jesuits. The Greek MONOS from which came Monk means *alone, isolated*. From there comes what the scholars have called *mon'-archy* the government of one only! Now the Jesuits strictly call themselves MONOS or *monk* so that their *archaios* or *archee* or *arche* who presides over them, if they ever consolidate a foot on the earth, is by its nature and in all antiquity the true MONOS, the MON'-ARCHAIOS, the *mon'-arch* of the universe. This is how titles are prepared! It is only about being the strongest to make them respected; one *works at it*: *e piano, piano si và lontano*.

It is the order that gives the *attire*: this is why the apron is called the *attire*.

The explanation given in lodge on the reasons of the nudity of the *heart* and the *knee* is correct. The gender of the person receiving the reception must be convincing, because a woman can never be a *Jesuit*, nor *work* like a Jesuit. As the good fathers say, "but none but *Males* shall know my Mind."[132]

Upon the reception of the *profane*, one makes him put a shoe *in slipper*. This is to symbolize Ignatius of Loyola: he left barefoot from Montserrat for his *pilgrimages*; but suffered an injury to one of his feet and put a sandal on that foot.[133]

The recipient is introduced in the lodge by two hurried knocks on the door followed by another very slow one. Sometimes, to lead the observer astray, it is one distinct knock followed by two hurried ones. The knock stricken slowly is to *command* the attention in lodge: the two hasty knocks are the true Jesuitical sign, the sign of the column B. There are two knocks to

---

[131] Open Father Jouvency, Jesuit, in his *Greek roots*, page 301, *catholicos, universal*, root Olos *all*.

[132] See *Masonry Dissected* p. 165.

[133] See also in *La fleur des saints*, the life of Saint Ignatius written by a Jesuit. [SE: *Lives of the Saints*, probably *Flos Sanctorum* by Father Ribadeneira. Voir *Notices littéraires sur le dix-septième siècle* par Léon Aubineau, Ch. XI. Le P. de Ribadeneira. 1859].

indicate this sacramental B, the second letter of the alphabet. It is also to remember their two great Saints *Ignatius* and *Xavier* and their *two* patrons *Come* and *Damien* that the Jesuits give two small knocks from a finger into the hand when they want to question and to recognize themselves.

The journeys are borrowed from the Rosicrucians, but for the Jesuits they symbolize their *missions* that were at all times the great object of their order: they were busy preaching a mission in England when they gained entry into Masonry, and when they made of the *literary society* of the Rosicrucian Masons an *order* of celibate monks.

The apprentice takes three steps to approach the master and to take the oath at the altar. These three steps allegorically express the three vows of the *externals*; X^{um}, or professed of the three oaths, *exteri seu professi trium votorum*.

He is then guided to the column I, this letter I is the ninth letter of the alphabet. The number 9 gives three times three, the sacred number of Jesuitized Freemasons. To force them to greet by nine or three times three, it is specifically ordering them to salute the column I, that is to salute one another by Saint Ignatius I!

Saint Ignatius came to Paris with two partners to have his order approved. Nine partners joint him in Paris for the establishment of *his company*. This number nine was probably adopted in the manner of the order of the Templars.

Would it not be the Jesuits who placed nine enormous angels around the *Trinity* Column in Vienna? There are other angels there as well, but those only symbolize a *company* of swift and ready angels.

Philosophi Incogniti – P.I – that is *patres jesuitae*, Jesuit Fathers. *Ordo Interior* means *Ordo Jesu*.

In the book *Des Erreurs et de la Vérité* [Of Errors and Truth] the new Prophet is called the Philosophe Inconnu –P.I – *Pater Jesuita*.

The passwords have not been chosen *lightly*. *Jachin* means, according to the public explanation of all lodges: *"My strength is in God."* Now we know the God of the Jesuits; it is their General.

The *lodge* of Saint John means the *college* of Saint-Ignatius.

One speaks in the lodges of hundred cannons on St. John's Island: these *cannons* must announce the great power of the Jesuits.[134]

The apprentice is called *Tubalcain*. It is quite strange to call the *apprentice* Tubalcain, since he has been stripped of all his metals. Tubalcain, according to the Genesis, is the first who worked on metals. A Tubalcain without metals is therefore not a Tubalcain: the allegory is correct according to the

---

[134] [SE: I could not find a direct reference for the one hundred cannons. However, it may be an allusion to the company of the one hundred associates, created by Richelieu to help establishing the Colony of Quebec. There is indeed a St John's Island in Quebec, now known as Prince Edward Island.]

meaning of the Jesuits. The apprentice is not a *Tubalcain* T, but a *temporal* T, or a Jesuit of the first degree.

The fellow craft companion is called *Shiboleth*, because of the letter S, which must be the emblem of the *scholasticus* S, the scholastic or Jesuit of the second profession. In several lodges a *blue* ribbon is attached to his apron: azure *blue* is the favorite color of the order. Their number I H S, [135] that is to say, *Jesum habemus socium, we have Jesus as our companion*, is placed on an azure background, because the sun against the azure sky is the emblem of the Jesuits.

The number S. S. J. or *socius societatis Jesu*, fellow of the Society of Jesus, is literally the Jesuit *companion*; he receives the word *Schiboleth* – S – from the Jesuits for his name of *Scholastic*. To reveal to him allegorically that he is a priest, one gives him for *sign* a grip *on the middle finger*, and he is told that it is because of the *Middle Chamber* of Salomon's temple.

"Where did your receive your wages" says the Fellowcraft catechism, which is printed everywhere by the way.

"In the Middle Chamber."

Now it was in the *Middle Chamber* that the priests of the temple of Jerusalem consumed the sacrificial meats.

The G in the Blazing Star is not shown to the apprentice; it is only shown in the next degree because the apprentice Mason, or first professed Jesuit, begins his entry into the order only at the second professed level, or fellowcraft.

In the past, music was produced during the reception of a Fellow Craft, because he then begins to be a Jubal, called musician by the Holy Scriptures. This *Jubal* I means nothing else but Jesuit.

The seven steps that the Fellow Craft has to climb are for him the emblem of the seven sacerdotal ordinations.

His three steps mean, like the three steps of the Apprentice, the *professed of the three vows*.

The B of the column shown to him symbolizes the number two.

The G shown to him at the same time, symbolize a number seven.

The B, the second letter of the alphabet, and the G, the seventh, give together the number nine, or I, that is to say, Jesuit: the Fellow Craft Macon, or Scholastic of the second Jesuitic profession, receives expressly here the Jesuit name, because he just entered in the order.

In the Perfect Elect Mason, Salomon hits seven strokes very slowly to express the G, the *General*, and the Master Hiram adds *two strokes* hastily, to express that he is the General of the Company of the Jesuits.

---

[135] [SE: The monogram "IHS" was originally an abbreviation of the first three letters in Greek of the name "Jesus": "IHCOYC" (The "S" for "C" is an attempt to deal with the Greek letter "Sigma". Later, various meanings were derived in Latin for the letters: "Jesus Hominum Salvator" (Jesus, Savior of Men); "In Hoc Signo Vinces" (In this sign, you shall conquer); "Jesum Habemus Socium" (We have Jesus as our Companion) are a few of them.]

2. Masonry and Company of Jesus

The tracing board of the Philosophes Inconnus Apprentices depicts on the triangular-shaped carpet the letters:

J X

B

So the B is placed in such a way that it relates as much to the I as to the X.[136]

B means *Beatus*. Therefore the purpose of the triangle is to express *Beatus Ignatius, Beatus Xaverius*.

As for the letters G, A, J, N, these are the four Jesuitical letters already mentioned, *generalis, assistentes, jesuitae, nostri*.

But the N is in front of the X: the N means the *Nosters*; the X means the X^I, that is, *exteri* or *external*.

Under the N figure four points and the number 2 in this manner :: 2. These four points are the explanation of the letter N: they express the four vows of the Jesuit Ours – N – or professor of the four vows, *nostri, seu professi quatuor votorum*,:: The number 2 expresses the order of the Jesuits.

Under the X there are three points and the number 7 in this manner 7 ∴. These three points recall the profession of the three vows, that is to say, X^I., abbreviation of exteri or external or professors of the three vows. As for the numbers 2 and 7, they represent B and G, second and seventh letters of the alphabet, whose total gives 9 or the letter I, Ignatius and Jesuit.

A certain Mr. de Woechter, whose manuscript titled *Œuvres magiques*[137] runs by the world, speak of these numbers in a very expressive, although mysterious, manner. He says in his *Œuvres magiques*: "The one who is not of the number 7 and 2 does not possess the watchword. The magic of Mr. Woechter can be explained without being a great wizard. The one who doesn't know that 7 and 2 make 9 and represent the ninth letter of the alphabet I, doesn't know the *Jesuitic Magnum Opu*; he doesn't know that he is a Jesuit.

---

[136] See the book titled *Les Apprentis Philosophes Inconnus*. [SE: This is about the chapter and the figure having the same name found in Tschoudy's l'*Étoile Flamboyante*, Volume 2.]

[137] [SE: Possibly *Magische Werke*, possibly Leonhard von Wächter (1762-1837) or Carl Eberhard von Wächter (1746-1825)].

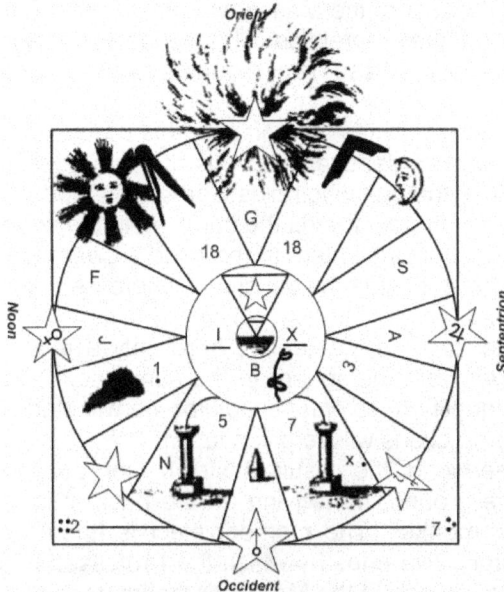

[Figure 3 –Tracing board of the Philosophes Inconnus Apprentices][138]

Close to the circle, in the middle of the same tracing board figure the numbers 1, 7, 5, 13, 18. These numbers, reduced in letters, mean *agents*.

Between these numbers one sees in a triangle a F with the numbers 5 and 3. The letter F is only placed there to represent allegorically the number 6. The total of these three numbers 6, 5 and 3 give the number 14, or the fourteenth letter of the alphabet or O. This O is the common abbreviation of the word *ordo*, order. As a whole, this numeric triangle means ORDO AGENS, *acting order*.

The symbols of the Master Degree have been borrowed from the conjuration formed by the friends of Charles I to revenge his death, and to put his son on the throne. The Jesuits easily created from it the gloomy ceremonies of an ecclesiastic order, from the time a novice publically professes his vows. The shroud, the corpse, the *Miserere*, death psalm, the coffin of Hiram-Abif, everything is ghastly there.

This Hiram-Abif, H and A replace here the letters B and G of Fellow craft's Degree; they come back to the same and also represent the number nine or the Jesuit letter I.

The letter H is for the number 8; the letter A is for the number 1; total 9 or Jesuit. We already showed that B, the second letter, and G, the seventh of the alphabet, give the dedicated number nine, or the Jesuit letter I.

---

[138] [SE: This Figure adapted from Tschoudi, and given here as example, does not entirely correspond to Bonneville's description.]

2. Masonry and Company of Jesus

H and A form the number of the Mason who arrives at the mastery; B and G form the number of the apprentice who becomes a fellow craft. While different in appearance, these two numbers also express that they are Jesuits.

Above the corpse lying down in the coffin, an I *is watching.* It is explained by the past word of *Master*, Jehovah; there is the *true Jesuit*, The one that is God's representative, the one who holds God's place, *locum Dei tenens.*

The apprentice, or *temporal,* guards the column I in the square of the temple; the *companion*, or *scholastic* enters in the *Middle Chamber*, and the master, or *spiritual coadjutor*, comes in the sanctuary where he makes his profession. He dies for the world.

The three steps toward the Master are here only a repetition of the three vows; he steps over from the square to the compass, or from obedience to command. In his quality of *spiritual coadjutor*, he will start assisting the *God* of the order; some functions will be given to him.

While dying for the world, the Jesuit Master Mason does not have his face turned towards the ground; he is lying on the back; it is to distinguish him from the *common* monks. The member elect is [then] raised by the five points of the mastery; five grips by which the Professed hugs and holds the new Master. Up to the grip of the Master or the impression of the five fingers spread out, "everything here complies with the reception of the spiritual coadjutor in the order of the Jesuits."

The password *chiblim* – C –, which represents the spiritual coadjutor, is explained in the catechisms with lots of finesse. The catechism explains that these *chiblim* are stone carvers who knew how to prepare their materials with such precision that the architect could build while neither hammers nor axes would be heard in the surroundings. Could someone express better the silence, and the secret of the Jesuitical work?

The new Master word *Mac Benac* is explained by the widow's son, or Charles II, son of the widowed queen. This Charles II is the *lost word* sought by the Masons. Here we note that the Greek word Logos not only means *verb*, or *speech*, but also *son*[139]: therefore they looked for the *son* of Charles I who was lost.

In addition, the word *Mac-Benac* symbolizes THE ORDER by its two capital letters; - M - 12, B - 2, that is 14; the number 14 gives the letter O, *ordo.* In this way the literary society of Bacon was changed in an *order.*

And since the correct word of this degree is Ihevoah I or *Jesuit*, the set of the letters M, B and I expresses *ordo jesuitarum*, the order of the Jesuits.

---

[139] [SE: "Son" is not a direct translation of the term logos λόγος. On the other hand, the conception that the Christ is the Logos has been important in the establishment of the doctrine of the divinity of Jesus Christ and his position as God the Son in the Trinity. For an interesting analysis of the logos, see Reed's article, *How Semitic Was John? Rethinking the Hellenistic Background to John 1:1.* Anglican Theological Review, Fall 2003.]

The word *Jehovah* has been made a password: a word that must be *hidden*. This is again an allegory to express that no one must know the true name of the Masons.

The Masons themselves according to the catechism must look for the name that belongs to them.

The master killed in the new system signifies the order of the Jesuits; the three companions who killed him toward the East, the South and the North, are the three kingdoms; England, Scotland, and France, from where the Jesuits have been ordered out in the beginning of the sixteenth century; these three kingdoms are located exactly in the East, South and North.

The body of the Master Hiram, following their modern allegorical *lectures* or *legends*, was looked for by nine Masters; the older catechism says that the body of Hiram was looked for by fifteen Masters, which comes back to the same. 9 is J or *jesuitae*, Jesuits. 15 gives P *patres*, Jesuit Fathers. There are three times three knocks, or nine, because the three vows are perfect.

These three Jesuitical degrees are given in the temple, but the fourth vows; or the profession of the *Ours* is given secretly, and can only be pronounced after having reached 45 years![140]

The fourth degree of the Masonry is the Scottish Mastery. It functions as an emblem of the fourth vow of the *Ourrs* in the order of the Jesuits. But how terrifying is the image that the Scottish Masonry gives us about the fourth profession of the Jesuits? Their first sign is. .... A sign of terror. It is the last shout of the nature over which one wants to triumph. The dagger is raised. One is quiet, what a silence! A dark lantern casts intermittently a pale light that is going to mark the victim. The *brotherly* word is *vengeance*! And it is against my homeland that the Superior Inconnus pronounced it! I don't know if it is indignation or fright that, at the sight of so many horrors, has a grip on me. What is therefore the blood that Masons need to spread! – Cowards! The quill falls of the hands.

The four steps of this degree represent four vows of the *Our*, and the five emblematic animals of the carpet, represent the five points the mastery.

The steps make 4. The animals make 5. 5 after 4 makes 45, it is the age of a *noster* or *Our*. Compare this explanation with the Jesuitical book titled: *of Errors and Truth.*[141]

It is in the hieroglyphs of the Jesuit Tipotius,[142] that the Superior Inconnus took their five allegorical animals: the pelican, the eagle, the lion, the fox and the monkey.

No animal in everything can shine.[143]

---

[140] See the decoding of the word Mason, p. 84.

[141] [Possibly, Louis-Claude of Saint-Martin. *Des Erreurs et de la Vérité* (Of Errors and Truth). 1775.]

[142] See again Jacob Typot, or Jacques Typoets, also called Jacobus Tipotius. Symbola divina et humana pontificum imperatorum regum. Accessit brevis, et facilis isagoge.

2. Masonry and Company of Jesus

The various properties of the five animals are the emblem of the five qualities required from the General of the Jesuits. In the Strict Observance, the eagle is called *sparrow hawk*, and the pelican is rejected.

The Scottish [Masters] hit by four times four, it is the perfection of the cubic *ashlar*, or of an *Our*. Additionally, for the Scottish Master to be the absolute emblem of an *Our*, the former catechism gives him the name of Natumad. N. *Noster Our*.

In the hymns of the Freemasons one sings there: *Mason Noah, Most Worshipful*; and the Masons are called *children of Noah, N. noster, Our*. Additionally Noah's ark is found on several carpets of Scottish Masonry. The ark has always been the symbol of a church or blessed assembly, *beatorum*. The Jesuits accepted it as emblem of happiness prepared to their order. There, instead of the Blazing Star, is found the lion of the tribe of Judah, with its *blazing* sword. The Jesuits pretend to originate from this tribe. JESU-ITA literally means 'who walks on Jesus' steps'. It is to walk from rather far away. The Superior Inconnus don't allow their Scottish initiates to pronounce the consecrated word of this degree out of the lodges; the word is JEHOVAH. There is a double allegory here. The Scottish Masons must be Jesuits without knowing it, and it must not be known that they are Jesuit.

In the past century Masonry was limited to these four degrees, and it is clear that they correspond to the four vows of the professions of the Jesuits. In these four degrees, the order of the Freemasons was precisely what it had to be to fulfill the views of its founders, its fathers, and Superior Inconnus.

All lower and higher degrees established later offer nothing *new*; all are explained by the ancient catechisms; they are only the results of fear. The Superior Inconnus promised so many times to unveil to the Mason brethren the greatest secrets, that the initiates, always blind and well stocked, wanted to know finally if they were not also driven by blinds or impostors. The deceivers had to resort to new fuss. Our century saw the mysterious birth of a crowd of beautiful inventions; but the Superior Inconnus always remained behind the curtain.

We are going to indicate the main periods of the *re-Creation* of the same allegories under other shapes, from the time Masonry was incorporated *as an order of monks* to the order of the Jesuits.

In 1688, William, prince of Orange, made a coming down in England: the following year he was proclaimed king. In 1690, Jacques II being defeated, the Jesuits; who lost all their expectations in England, ran away in France with their dethroned king. The Jesuit Jacques II stayed at the college of Clermont, famous college of the Jesuits. This was when this college produced the acts, the orders and the new institutes that governed the Masonic world.

---

[143] La Fontaine. [*Fables*. The Peacock complaining to Juno Book II].

In France, it was the *Order of Masonry*, that is, the Order of Jesuits. In the rest of Europe, it was only *Masonry*; a difference that the Jesuit writers take great care to mark in their writings.

If King William, in 1693, was made Mason, as their calendar states, it is not an incredible thing. It is known that one can be made Mason without having anything to do with Jesuitism. Voltaire himself died Jesuit: did he have the least suspicion of it? Thus, while King William and other great men were been made Masons, it is not less true than the plan of Jesuitical Masonry is to submit all kings to their General, the representative of God.

Queen Anne, the last of the House of Stuart, began to age. Toward the end of her reign, all conspired to make her favorable to the Pretender. The Duke of Marlborough fell into disfavor: like her, the Pretender descended from the House of Stuart. FRANCE WAS INTERESTED FOR HIM. The Queen declared the Pretender as her successor: The Jesuits were not idle. The Pretender was a toy between their hands. Under the shelter of his name, they made themselves partisans. Protestant or catholic, all was good for them to succeed. This is the event that gave birth to the degree of *Scottish of Scotland*, or *Scottish* [master] *of Saint Andrew*. The Pretender's partisans had to carry this degree publicly if he became king. This is when Masonry experienced zeal and *commotion*.

In the Strict Observance the Scottish is received rope about the neck, and he is shown skeletons of malefactors. This allegorical ceremony symbolizes all Protestants, who, not yet being in the hands of the Jesuits, were considered as parties guilty of high-treason. However they were graced by the *law of England that forgave then a priest who knew how to read and to write*.

In [French-spoken] lodges, these words *by benefit of clergy* are translated as *à cause de vos connaissances*. This impertinent translation falsifies history, is contrary to the English legislation, and puts mystery and charlatanism in a kind of knowledge that the last of the people would blush not to have.

The Protestants who, in the Jesuitical temple, swore faith and homage to the Pretender their slaves, were, at their initiation, watched like malefactors who had betrayed their legitimate king. One made them feel, before attaching the Saint-Andrew's Cross on them, that they had to receive his goodness for the remission of their high-treason crime.

The Pretender was supposed to grant them their grace, because they *knew how to read and write*. Therefore, it was not because of their mysterious knowledge.

The English law that forgave those who knew how to read and write was called *benefit of clergy*, the *privilege of the clergy*, or *happiness reserved to the clergy*. Then the Jesuits were this clergy. The Scottish must *symbolize* this clergy: the Jesuits at the time of the establishment of their order were called the *clergy* or *the clerks of the Society of Jesus, clerici societatis Jesu*.

In 1715 the Pretender disembarked in Scotland. He was beaten, and had to run away in France the following year. Then the famous degree became useless. But to sustain the blinding of Freemasons, it was recomposed for another purpose.

2. Masonry and Company of Jesus

The House of Brunswick and Lüneburg was becoming stronger on the throne of England. The Jesuits, their ecclesiastical scheming, their customs and their despotism became odious. The calendar of the Freemasons speaks of an important assembly, held in England, July 24 1720. It is said that precious documents were burnt then as they could have unveiled the great secret.[144]

These Masons, who assembled were the Jesuits, Masters *of the Masonry whose existence was not suspected by the public*. Then the existence of a Frey-masonry was spread everywhere. It was spoken about as a marvelous thing, as a treasure of all wisdom of the ancients. This step was indispensable for the Jesuits to prepare secret assemblies, to draw partisans to them, to choose among them at leisure, and to gain lots of money by admitting profanes.

People would go successively through the four degrees or four receptions and leave the temple as *blind* as they came in. And the *golden veal* that they *incensed* and *worshiped* and *canonized* was soon no more that a poor wretch, a god *without gilding*, a veal without silver thrown to rubbish.

The Masonic calendar proves that the expansion of Masonry was seriously considered as soon as 1718.

Numerous lodges were established in 1721 and in 1722 in London. The *Book of Constitutions* was published in the year 1723.

On page 54 of this Book of Constitutions it is said that "all Mason must be of the catholic religion."[145] But this Jesuitical catholicity is far from looking like the Catholicism of Christians, since the English anti-Catholics are the most zealous Masons; unless one suspected the greatest men of England not to have known how to read what was written expressly in the *public* Book of Constitutions of Masonry.

As we saw above, Masonry existed in its strength within the college of Clermont in Paris. However, no one in France, with the exception of the initiates, had the slightest idea about the existence of this Masonry. After announcing Masonry in England through the *Book of Constitutions*, they let hardly two years go by, and then an English Lord, called Derwentwater, pretended to bring it in France for the first time. It was indeed the first time that it was known there *publicly*. After this great endeavor, Lord

---

[144] [SE: See *The Constitutions of the Ancient and Honourable Fraternity of Free and Accepted Masons*. Published by John Entick in 1767, more commonly known as *Anderson's Constitutions of 1738*. p. 191. "This Year, as some *private* Lodges, several very valuable Manuscripts (for they had nothing yet in Print) concerning the Fraternity, their Lodges, Regulations, Charges, Secrets, and Usages, (particularly one writ by Mr Nicholas Stone, the Warden of *Inigo Jones*) were too hastily burnt by some scrupulous Brothers, that those Papers might not fall into strange Hands."]

[145] [SE: "we being only, as Masons, of the Catholick Religion above-mention'd".]

Derwentwater, partisan of the Pretender was beheaded in London for crime of high treason.[146]

The French, always kind because they are always human, could not be satisfied a long time with mysterious assemblies, where funeral ceremonies and some daggers soon showed them bloody conjurations and some cowardly vengeance that would offend them. They were first given a moral interpretation. It is for them alone that the inventions of the blackest politics were *puerilized*. The banquet, the songs, the *strong powder, the triple fire, the canons, the barriques,*[147] and all innocent board games, come from France. This childishness is again a new feature of the politics of the Jesuits: For sixty years, they served to divert the public attention in France. The French even wanted a Masonry for women; and in spite of the Superior Inconnus, they created a Masonry for women. They call these lodges of women *adoption lodges*: and since they usually gathered the elite of the court and the city, all French Masons run to these lodges of adoption and to their benefits. Our French embarrass themselves little of the screams of some Masons in a bad mood, who assure them daily that Masonry would be never anything *in France*, as long as women are admitted into it. They call them pedants; and persuaded that if a real secret existed in Masonry, it would have been known a long time ago. Their entire Masonic knowledge is limited to the signs of admission and all their speeches in lodges are only exhortations, often quite eloquent, to rescue the brethren or the unhappy travelers, and to drink in chorus to the health of the sisters who adorn their banquet.

To keep their goal, and to keep it always hidden, the Superior Inconnus had to invent a new symbolic language. To conquer Palestine, meant in the *Inner* Sanctuary to change the religion of England; the last crusades symbolized the unhappy attempts of the Pretender; the islands of Scotland represented emblematically Paris, situated in the island of France; *Mount* Heredom symbolized the college of Cler'-Mont; the construction of the first temple represented the establishment of the college of the Jesuits that Jacques II made build when he was duke of York; the construction of the second temple by Jerubabel I, was the emblem of the relationship of the Jesuits with the Pretender. The English were called the prisoners jailed in Babylon. The Pretender had to be the modern Cyrus, and he would be leading them in Palestine to build the new temple of Jerusalem there. This is the simple explanation of the allegories that are the general basis of all high Masonic Degrees.

---

[146] [SE: First Grand Master of the Order of France, he died decapitated in 1746].

[147] [SE: Those terms used during the banquets, or *table lodges*, of French Masons. The strong powder refers to wine, the triple fire to the three sequences of the third toast, the canons to glasses and the barriques to bottles.]

2. Masonry and Company of Jesus

No Jesuit was more zealous than the Scottish *Ramsay* to establish the new system. For this, he wrote the *Travels of Cyrus*[148] for the Pretender's eldest son. He makes him take the solemn oath to build to the Lord ([in French, Seigneur] - S *societati*), a house in the City of Jerusalem in Judea, when he will be the master of the East (that is to say England located in the east) upon his entry in Babylon (that is in London).

The seven degrees of the new system were published in 1766 under the title of *High Degrees of Masonry*. The first three degrees of the *Elect* aim at the vengeance of the assassins of the Master Hiram; without the need for allegory this is the order of the Jesuits. There, all is dagger and murder and vengeance. The three degrees that follow aim at the construction of a second temple; the seventh [degree] or Noachite is the perfect vow of the Ours, among whom the Jesuits choose their General.

In the year 1730 Ramsay went to England to introduce the new system there. His zeal caused some concerns; he didn't find that all Masons were ready to pay for the two guineas that he required to give his degrees there. The order succeeded better in France than Ramsay did in England. [Masons] were committed to pay ten Louis d'or per year. Ramsay said in a printed speech, but very rare today, that he hoped to gather from all Masonic contributions thirty thousand Louis per year, *for the main goal of Masonry*. This confession, full of candor was taken then for a mysterious goal; but the thirty thousand Louis, given by the initiates, was really *the main goal of Masonry*. The ducat of Saint John, or annual free financial gift, or donation of Saint Ignatius, still required in some lodges of Germany, doesn't have a nobler origin.

One didn't stick a long time to these high Degrees. It was always necessary to make a step further toward the hidden goal of the Superior Inconnus. The first Degree invented to draw a greater number of partisans, was a magic Masonry system established in Florence. Soon after some fragments of the former symbols of the Rosicrucian Masons were added to it.

In the *Art Royal du Chevalier Rose-Croix*,[149] the initiates in lodges wear the *attire of the holy office*. In the Middle Chamber they are served with bread

---

[148] [SE: Ramsey. *Les voyages de Cyrus, Avec un Discours Sur La Mythologie* (Paris, 1727). Translated as *The travels of Cyrus to which is annex'd a discourse upon the theology & mythology of the pagans* (London, 1728). This book composed in avowed imitation of Fenelon's *Adventures of Telemachus* as indicated in an anonymous pamphlet *Entretiens sur les Voyages de Cyrus* (1728)]. This is actually probably the source of Voltaire's entry 'Plagiarism" in his *Dictionnaire Philosophique*: "In these travels, he [Ramsay] copies the sentences, reasoning of an ancient English author who introduces a young solitary man dissecting his dead sheep, and going back to God through his sheep. This strongly resembles plagiarism. But by leading Cyrus in Egypt, he uses, to describe this singular country, the same expressions used by Bossuet; he copies him word by word without citing him. This is here plagiarism in all its forms.".]

[149] [*Royal Art of the Rose Croix Knight*] printed in London in 1770.

and wine to symbolize the Eucharist or the Holly Communion, in imitation of Christ; and all this, to pretend to have a reasonable goal. The third innovation was an order of Templars that they pretended to renew in France. This order was called the Strict Observance, to facilitate a means to bring back the Masons to patience and to advise them to arm themselves somehow, under a dangerous hope to take back their considerable goods from the crowns that stripped them. *It was also about giving importance to their symbols, and about bringing to understanding the necessity to respect the veil that hid the Superior Inconnus.*

In the famous book titled *Imago Primi Soeculi*, [150] I P S to express allegorically *jesuitarum patrum societas*, society of the Jesuit Fathers, the terrifying Ignatius of Loyola is represented like an enterprising man who only dreamed of battles, tournaments and knighthood. He spoke of the Christ like a General of army; he called the society a COMPANY, because blind obedience is the first discipline of the military art.

In this image of the society of the Jesuit fathers the entire order is symbolized on page 52 by a knight fully armed on an impetuous messenger; on page 328 a *ring* is the emblem *of the vocation to the order.* One must with a *short spear* carry away the ring. Thousands of Freemasons would not have suspected in the picture of the society of the Jesuit fathers, the origin mysterious of their beloved ring.

[Figure 4 - No is mortale quod opto. What I desire is not mortal. *Imago*. P. 52.]

---

[150] *Imago primi saeculi Societatis Iesu a Provincia Flandro-Belgica eiusdem Societatis repraesentata ...* Antuerpiae: Ex officina Plantiniana Balthasaris Moreti (Image of the First Century of the Society of Jesus, refered to in this work as The *Imago Primi Soeculi*), 1640.

[Figure 5 - Terram deservisse iuvat. *Imago*. P. 328.]

Lessing in his *Nathan the Wise*[151] drew skillfully the Templar's character: he made allusion there to Masonic signs and to the mysterious ring. From the nervous tone of that section of his writing, we can be sure that he believed he was a true Templar and that he ignored the real significance of the Jesuitical ring: because far from being written to establish only one religion, the whole piece of Lessing announces a beneficent sage who preaches the universal tolerance. This is what makes me understand now why the Germans, who make a great business of the Masonry, look at *Nathan the Sage* as the first of their *dramatic* master pieces: there are few who don't know this play by heart. From all sides people were telling me about this famous play, about translating it and also about the impossibility to have it adequately translated by a *Frenchman*. For me who was not a Mason, I could only find things that were too strong for censorship, and yet *it was necessary to say everything*, because one shouted to me all the time: *Oh the ring! The ring will make noise in France! Don't spoil my ring.*[152] Unfortunately the play, although of a great merit was received rather coldly: a very mediocre comedy was preferred to it. In addition, the ring was not mentioned. "The French", said the Germans in their *critiques*", are not *instructed* enough to know the merit of this admirable play, the pearl of the tragedies of the great Lessing."

Observe while passing that the taste of a nation for some works should not be judged lightly; and that it is more difficult to explain an allegory than to find it absurd, like these small industrious knights

---

[151] [SE: Drama poem in five acts and in verses, *Nathan the Wise* was written by the German Gotthold Ephraim Lessing (1729-1781) between November 1778 and March 1779. A fervent plea for religious tolerance, it describes the bridging of gaps between Judaism, Islam and Christianity. Its performance was forbidden by the church during Lessing's lifetime and banned by the Nazis. The centerpiece of the work is the Ring Parable.].

[152] The ring of the fifth act should not be confused with the parable of the rings of the *Decameron* by Boccaccio that Lessing placed in the first acts of the tragedy.

Who by *Voltairizing* themselves as lords of learning,
Hurry to teach what they didn't learn.

Compare the history of the alleged great masters with the history of the Generals of the Jesuits; it is absolutely the same history under other names. France, England and Italy were already taken in the traps of the Jesuits. Germany was still free. The close friend of Ramsay, who lived then in Frankfort, undertook to establish a universal hierarchy.[153] And this goal of the friend of Ramsay is so Jesuitical, that today the Jesuits work *secretly* and *publicly* to build the altar of their OMNIPOTENCE.[154] In *L'Étoile flamboyante*, [155] Jesuitical book, the knights of the holy City must defend the religion.

Against whom? I pray you.

Germany having been prepared by a book published in Frankfurt on the Main, [156] the Jesuits hurried to transport the Strict Observance there. 'To restore the strict observance' is a dedicated expression used while speaking of an order *that moved away from the former rule.*
The King of Prussia Frederick II, some time after his accession to the throne, had a lodge of Freemasons established in Berlin. It gave birth to several others. They all were inconsequential *until the Seven Years' War.* The Marquis de Bernez, who was then among the prisoners of war, communicated mysteriously to the Worshipful of the lodge of Berlin the new idea of an order of Templars. He wrote P.C. allegorically to hide the name of the Grand Master. He dared explaining him this allegory by the name of Prince of Clermont P.C. The real words, hidden under the emblem of these two initial letters, are *patres claromontani*, fathers of the college of Clermont P.C. Taking advantage of the name of a very great prince, the Jesuits easily made their supposed system of Templars adopted. It now spreads like a torrent in all Europe under the very innocent name of the Strict Observance.
The domination of the Jesuits became shaky. From 1762 until 1764 where one worked courageously to expel them from Spain and France, they

---

[153] See the works of Loen [SE: It is probably about Johann M. von Loen who wrote among others, *La véritable Religion, unique dans son espèce, universelle dans ses principes, corrompue par les disputes des théologies, divisée en plusieurs sectes, réunies en Christ.* Francfort, 1751, 2 vol. in-8 and *Système de religion universelle.* 1753 in-8].
[154] It is the proper word of a ceremony of their Superior Degrees.
[155] [SE: Probably *L'Étoile flamboyante, ou la Société des Francs-Maçons, considérée sous tous ses aspects.* Théodore-Henri de Tschudi, Charles Louis Bardou-Duhamel. Frankfurt, 1776, 2 vol. in-12]
[156] It has for title *l'histoire des Francs-Maçons.* [SE: Maybe, the *Histoire, obligations et statuts de la très vénérable confraternité des Francs-Maçons ...* Francfort sur le Mein, 1742].

doubled their efforts to spread secretly their new order of the Templars in all lodges. First a certain *Johnson* was used. He was an adventurer to their discretion. However, soon after for fear that the *machine* could betray the *artist* one day, *Johnson* was murdered at the Warteburg Castle. The history of this murder, that can be read handwritten in England, is frightening.

In this new system of Templars only six degrees are published. The seventh degree or *clerus* was held secret. Finally, it had to come out to pacify the impatience of the Masons; they were complaining with indignation that someone was deceiving them.

Always persecuted by Masons determined to see some titles, to calm them momentarily, the same system of Templars under another shape was given back to them. Zinnendorf[157] published his new Masonic System, where the seventh Degree *clerus* or *clerk* comes from Sweden. This *clerus* is called *favorite of Saint John,* F.S.J., to express by the initial letters, the real *clerk,* that is to say the *brother* of the Society of Jesus, *frater societatis Jesu.*

After the general establishment of a so-called order of the Templars, one took care of a system of *Rosicrucians, makers of gold.* The book of a sir Plumenoeck, [158] known under the title of *Compass of the Wise,* is nothing but *Rose-cross Magic.* The *Chapitre Illuminé (Enlightened Chapter* or *Grand Chapter*) is again the Company of Jesus.

All the way to France, this new system inspired cruel and atrocious fanaticism; "one cannot imagine this." Several unfortunates were seized, and delivered secretly to unimaginable tortures, to extract from their fresh blood, what they called the ARCHAEUS or the soul of nature. Without the intercession of a great prince the guilty parties might have suffered a pain different than that of exile. [159] There are crimes too dangerous to set an exemplary punishment!

The order of the Jesuits was close to be damaged in Germany. They published the *Étoile Flamboyante (Blazing Star)*; soon after the enigmatic book of *Des Erreurs et de la Vérité;* then *La Diadème des Sages* and the *Tableau naturel des rapports qui existent entre Dieu, l'homme et l'univers.*[160]

---

[157] [SE: Physician in chief and minister of the Emperor Charles VI. His system of Masonry was the extension of a rite called the Illuminés d'Avignon, established by Pernetti in 1760. He died in 1800, leaving behind him many new degrees of Masonry, and particularly a novel arrangement of the Chevalier du soleil].

[158] [SE: *Compass der Weisen,* or *Compass of the Wise,* first published in 1799. Authorship uncertain but may be Adam Michael Birkholz, under the pseudonym Ketmia Vere alias Plumenoeck.]

[159] See *Deutsches Museum,* Erndtemond 1782. [SE: Probably the periodical published in Leipzig by Boie and von Dohm].

[160] [SE: Onesime-Henri de Loos. *La Diadème des Sages, ou démonstration de la Nature inférieure; dans lequel on trouvera une analyse raisonnée du livre des Erreurs et de la Vérité.* Paris 1781. Saint-Martin. *Des erreurs et de la vérité* (1775). *Ode/Stances sur l'origine et la destination de l'homme*

These last three books have the same logic and will stop being illegible to those who will try to learn with us the favorite game of the Jesuits who have fun trying to deceive us. Translations of these Masonic works were made in all language. However the translators were not Jesuits. They destroyed the meaning hidden under the numbers and made of these ridiculous works an even more ridiculous chat.

Seeing that the French were pleased with their small game of princes of Jerusalem and Templars, and that they were very quiet, as long as they were to keep their *canons of strong powder*, their lodge of adoption, and the *alms-box*, the Superior Inconnus proceeded to destroy it in Germany, where one began to sustain that it was only child's game, established to hide another intention.

This is when a multitude of mystical books appeared: the *Stumbling Block*,[161] *On the goal of the order of the Freemasons*,[162] and *On the Mysteries of the Freemasons*.[163]

These books speak about very interesting things happening in the inside of the order, I.O. *Ordo Jesuitarum*. They preach the Superior Inconnus, S.I. *Societas Jesuitarum*. They assure that the *Ours* are the real Masons, that the order was perfect before Masonry came out of its author's hands, that the Jews and Freemasons were contradictory beings and that *castrati* and women could never enter in the secret of the Masons.

It was a last stroke of genius, and to change Masonry universally, and to make of it only a sad society of priests. Thus their anger against eunuchs and women who cannot become priests.

It was during the Masonic Congress of Wilhelmsbad, that the deputies of all lodges of Germany assembled. *The order of the Templars, as offered, was declared false and illusory*. However within the same Congress from this order of Templars is set into place an order of CHevaliers bienfaisants de la Cité Sainte C.H.B. (Knight Beneficent of the Holy City). This CHevalier Bienfaisant was announced in the book titled the *Blazing Star*.

What was therefore the goal of all these knighthoods? What is the relationship between a CHevalier bienfaisant de la Cité Sainte and the mysteries preached by Smith and others of the like? Was the good Adam also a CHevalier bienfaisant de la Cité Sainte? Let's count the numbers of the three letters in upper case that the Jesuits, who do nothing without intention, placed on the carpet as abbreviation of their new order. C H and B

(1781/96). 2. Reprint: Hildesheim 2001. 52/582 S. Leinen. Saint-Martin. *Tableau naturel des rapports qui existent entre Dieu, l'homme et l'univers* (1782). *Discours sur la meilleure manière de rappeler à la raison les nations livrées aux erreurs et aux superstitions* (1783).]

[161] *Stein des Anstosses*. [SE: Possibly *Stein des Anstosses und Fels der Aergerniss, alien meinen teutschen Mitbiirgern*. pp. 160. Gebruckt, 1780.].

[162] *Ueber die Geheimnisse des Frey-Maurer*.

[163] *Ueber Ueber den Zweck des Ordens der Frey-Maurer*. [SE: Possibly *Ueber den Zweck des Freymaurerordens* [anon.], Berlin]

give 3, 8, 2, making 13. The thirteenth letter of the alphabet is N. *Nostri.* Here they are again! Once again the *Ours!*

Let's say a word about the sir of Cagliostro and about his Egyptian Masonry, a true Masonic ruby.

When I was in London he published in a gazette the following code.[164]

> "To all True Mason. In the name of 9.5.8.14.20.1.8; - 9.5.18.20.18.
>
> "The time is at hand when the Building of the New temple, or New Jerusalem 3.8.20.17.8. must begin; this is to invite all True Masons in London, to join in the name of 9.5.18.20.18. (The only one, in whom is a divine 19.17.9.13.9.23.) To meet To-Morrow-Evening, the 3d instant 1786 (or 5790) at nine o'Clock, at Reilly's, great Queen-Street; to lay a plan for the laying the first stone of the foundation of the True 3.8.20.17.8. in this visible world, being the material representative temple of the spiritual 9.5.17.20.18.1.11.5.12.
>
> A MASON and member of the New 3.8.20.17.8."

In England where Masonry is not a child's game, this notice made a lot of noise. One wanted to know the author of the notice. It was the sir of Cagliostro.

In a Masonic Assembly efforts were gathered to find the wanted interpretation of it. One arrived there in a satisfactory manner.

All this Cagliostrian gossiping is again a same Jesuitical system, same source, same intention, pure quackery.

Let's start by changing the numbers into letters. We will read in the first seven numbers *Jehovah*; in the five next ones we will read the word *Jesus*.

> To all true Masons. In the name of Jehovah, Jesus.

Jehovah gives the letter I; Jesus gives the ninth letter or the jesuitic I again. So the first line of the Cagliostrian notice means merely:

> To all *true* or Jesuit Masons, in the name of Saint Ignatius I and the Jesuits I.

> "The time is at hand when the Building of the New temple, or New Jerusalem 3.8.20.17.8. *must begin.*"

The new temple N.T. means, masonically, the temple of the *Nosters, nostrorum templum* N.T.

The five numbers reduced in letters give chur(c)h. The new church of Jerusalem means explicitly the assembly of the Jesuits Ours. The Greek word that means church also means assembly.[165]

---

[164] See *Morning Herald*, Thursday November 2, 1786.

"This is to invite all True Masons in London, to join in the name of 9.5.18.20.18."

We gave the explanation of the English word MASON, written by a S. It is here written in the plural, to have a S besides, and can express the Ours of the Jesuitical society more clearly – N.S.[166]
The five numbers changed in letters give the name of Jesus J once again.

"The only one, in whom is a divine 19.17.9.13.9.19.23. To meet To Morrow-Evening, the 3d instant 1786 (or 5790) at nine o'Clock, at Reilly's, *great Queen-Street*; to lay a plan for the laying the first stone of the foundation of the True 3.8.20.17.8. in this visible world, being the material representative temple of the spiritual 9.5.17.20.18.1.11.5.12."

The first number of this paragraph gives the English word trinity, in French trinité.
This trinity is the *mysterious* word of the paragraph; because it doesn't mean here the *Jesus*, in who only Christians recognize a perfect *trinity*.
This triple number relates only to the word Chur(c)h, repeated three times in the paragraph; and so that one cannot be mistaken on the number *three*. He needed it *three times* to have a number *nine*, he forgot *three times* the second necessary C to write the word *church* correctly.
This triple omission of the C letter, the third letter of the alphabet, gives the number nine or the letter I. All these supposed Egyptian mysteries are only Jesuitism.
If we were to omit the letter C (and since it is omitted three times, it can be only a voluntary omission), it is to express the eternal secret of the new temple that must be kept by the Jesuits, who can only write symbolically the real name of the order.
The 5786 or 4000 years added to the first one thousand of the year of grace 1786 is a date adopted in general by the whole Masonry. This is not there a Cagliostrian innovation.
The four thousand years before Christ's birth are added to bring back innocently the origin of Masonry to the birth of the world. But instead of 5786, the sir of Cagliostro wrote 5790.
The Jesuits added the number 4 to the precise date of every year, to express the 4 vows of their order that appropriated Masonry.

---

[165] [SE: Ecclesia or ekklesia (ἐκκλησία) refers to, among others, church, congregation, assembly.]
[166] See the decoding of the word MASON, p. 84.

2. Masonry and Company of Jesus

From 5790 remove a number 4 :: you will have 5786. I never saw in France a Masonic date to which someone dared adding the 4 :: points of the Jesuitical mastery.

The third number of the Cagliostrian paragraph gives a second time the word Chur(c)h, of which the letter C has been removed, the third of the alphabet, and the symbol of the number 3.

The fourth number of the paragraph gives Jerusalem. The spiritual temple of *Jerusalem* I is therefore only the temple of Jesuitism. The paragraph is signed:

"A MASON and member of the New 3. 8. 20. 17. 8."

A MASON so written means a Jesuit OUR. These last numbers, reduced in letters, give, for the third time, the word Chur(c)h; and the C or number 3, is omitted again.

In this way the sir of Cagliostro is, of his own *avowal*, an Our, a member of the new church of Jerusalem, N.E.J. *nostrorum Jesuitarum ecclesia*.

Here is his *Great Work*, his philosophers' stone, his Golden Bough.

The *Royal Order* of H. R. D. M. *of Kilwinning in Scotland* is a more interesting phenomenon to explain, at this hour, than the alleged Egyptian Masonry of the sir of Cagliostro. I have at the moment under the eyes a proceeding of the college and Grand Chapter of this Royal Order. It *commands* that every knight of the Order, in order to enjoy the privileges and the kindness of the Scottish lodges, must register his name in the *sister* lodges, that is to say, in all lodges that depend from the Grand Chapter. He will be excluded from it if he doesn't want to take oath to observe punctually their statutes and orders. This proceeding is of March 11, 1783.

A *nota bene* specifies that all brethren who want to be initiated in these high degrees and who want their names registered on the registers of the order must contact ...[167]

"The very dear brother will receive the *initiation fee* and the registration."

The number and the symbols found in this proceeding emanated from the Heredomian throne specify quite well the nature and the object of this new Institute.

First all chapters and members of this society are addressed as if they are submitted and subjected to a college of the noble and royal order of the Knights Templars ℟.

---

[167] I wish to not disclose to the public indignation a man who could be honest, and the first victim of the Jesuitical charlatanism.

It is not here about a great lodge; it is about a college. The denomination is at least more expressive: evidently, it announces a new college of Cler'-Mount; Mount of the clergy or clerks.

The knights of this order are called Knights Templars ℗̶ for fear that they may be confused with the former Templars, enemies of the clergy.

This ℗̶ is a new game to express in a single figure the two initials of the words *patres jesuitae*, Jesuit Fathers.

These Templars ℗̶ offer again the same results as that of the CHevaliers Bienfaisants of the Holy City.

T, the nineteenth letter of the alphabet, and P, the fifteenth, give together 34.

The horizontal line that crosses the downstroke of ℗̶ must be taken as the prime number: join to this number 35 the number X, of which the *cross* on the leg of the letter ℗̶ is the emblem, you have for total 45, the age of an *Our*. There they are again!

These Templars ℗̶ are also called in the proceeding of the Grand Chapter of Heredom K.D.S.H., that is, members of the *society* of the D.... of Mount *Heredom* in Scotland, S.H.K.

It is easy to see that the D, the fourth letter of the alphabet, symbolizes here the four vows of an Our: there they are again under another shape. Now try to deny Pythagorean metempsychosis; different and always the same.

Above the letter H, the common abbreviation of the word Heredom, there should be the small cross † that symbolizes the society of the Jesuits. But this cross †, that would have betrayed them by raising a proud head, is placed *incognito* at the leg of the famous Templar ℗̶. The Fathers of Heredom were simply expressed by P H., one must carry the small cross attached to the foot of the Fathers ℗̶ to bring it to the order H. Then we obtain a well-known allegory P. H̶ – *patres jesuitae*.

The Templars ℗̶ greet one another by 72, 81, ... 3, 5, 7. *There they are again!* There they are again! 7 and 2 make 9, 8 and 1 also make 9. It is always the letter I or Jesuit. The four points express the four vows of the *ours*, and the other numbers give the letter P. or *patres*. It is rather natural that the *fathers* Ours greet another by the signs dedicated to the highest degree of their Company.[168]

The East of the Scottish Freemasons is marked by the words of Great East of H.R.D.M. As we see, this abbreviation gives all the initials of the syllables of He-ReDon-Mons, Mount HeReDom.

In this East reign S. V. P. – According to the Scottish interpretation, *silence*, *union* and *peace* reign on their dedicated mountain. According to the truth, it

---

[168] To all chapters and members of the college of the most noble and royal order of the Knight Templars ℗̶, of the seven and last degrees of all ancient and Masonry symbolic, extended all over the surface of the Earth. Greeting by 72, 81, ... 3, 5, 7.

2. Masonry and Company of Jesus

is the worshipful society of the fathers; who *reign* in these august residences, S.V.P. *societas veneranda patrum*.

The date of the proceeding is expressed as follows:

Common era: 17. – of the M, 57.

And of our B^n: $\dfrac{469}{1314}$

The number 1314 is the date of the death of Jacques Molay, last Grand Master of the Templars.

One put above this date the number   469,
because this number united to   1314,
give the precise date of their order,   1783.

The real date is on the first line. The number 17 expresses by abbreviation the year 1783, that is to say, the total of the two *lower* dates: but after the number 17 – or 1783, comes --- the common sign of subtraction; and the number that it is necessary to subtract is 57.

From   1783   Remains 1726.

Remove: 57

This last number is the date of their B^n. It was in 1726 that they finished the catechisms and Jesuitical rituals. Soon after they were published *symbolically* by Samuel Prichard.[169]

The tracing board that they put almost in front of the *act*, merits that we try to describe it in detail; because it tells more then one is accustomed to learn commonly in the universal society of the Freemasons.

The words *Metropolis of Scotland, College Heredon VII^d* engraved around the emblems can convince us that the Jesuits didn't at all give up their views on Great Britain. Even more, they suggest that the Jesuits *announce* sustained resolutions to build in the Capital of *Scotland* a Mountain Heredom to replace their college of *Cler'-Mont* absolutely ruined in Paris.

The middle of this tracing board displays a crowned sun. Its rays are visible on all sides although its front part is *hidden* behind the Masonic veils. I already showed that the sun was the emblem of the order of the Jesuits.

The crown of the sun has *seven tips,* each carrying a star. The seven tips give the G or the name of the General of the order, the *light* of the order, and the *god* of the order. Toward the left we see the *bird of the god throwing the thunder* in a proud attitude. Its eyes are turned toward the General and as if it waits for his wills to drop the thunderbolt on some proscribed head. The

---

[169] Masonry Dissected.

eagle of Jupiter is the emblem of a *royal order*, of a *divine order*. The goal of the order is to establish a *universal monarchy* that must be governed by the *hidden sun*. This goal of the order is declared on the right of the sun by a scepter with the globe of the world *appearing to be attached* on its extremity. The whole world must soon be only a game between the hands of the *Jesuit god*! And to express that he already governs it a little bit according to his will from an *invisible hand*, the hand of the scepter is hidden under the well prepared curtain of which it covered his face.

Behind the scepter we see the tower of a strong castle: it is a battlement tower. The tip of a spear rests on the tower while its shaft is *hidden* in the sphere of the sun. This emblem means that it is up to the sun to set into movement *everything that is locked* in the tower.
In front there is a broken *column*. Its capital and part of the shaft fell.
The inscriptions on this column are clearly explained with the help of the code adopted by the Jesuits.
The top of the *headless* shaft carries the following inscriptions:

> S. R. I.

That is to say, Societas *Regia Jesuitarum, Royal society of the Jesuits*.
Below the letter R there is a *beaming* triangle, emblem of the *Jehovah* or *sun*, itself the emblem of the General of the order.
This new symbol announces that *the same letters* must be transposed to read the General's title.

> R. S. J.

King of the *society* of the Jesuits. *Rex Societatis Jesuitarum*.
Below this *beaming triangle* we discover the known figure H symbolizing the Society of Jesus. This figure is explained again by another figure below: it is

a H topped by a A ($\overset{A}{H}$) that is to say, Hiram-Abif, the master killed, the order killed, *that still lives, that stands up, that asks for help*. H gives eight and A gives one, whose sum is the number nine or the letter I, of which in truth I am bored to write the Jesuitical significance I.
On the fallen shaft, below the capital, the famous – G –, or General, is engraved. Under the – G – are found the two initials that give by abbreviation the name *Beatus Ignatius*: these three letters are oriented as follows.

G

ᙠ   I

To express that the general must have the eyes attached on the society of the *Blissful Ignatius*, and that the Company of Saint Ignatius must absolutely not see anything but the general's order.
Toward the bottom part of the tracing board, always in the sphere of the sun, is a long dagger lain down on a palm leaf. It is the emblem of an *eternal* war, no peace to hope!
Between the palm leaf and the dagger one drew a ribbon banner whose extremities are split into *two*; the ribbon banner crosses the whole board.
In the right on the ribbon we read these demonic words, *God wants it!*
God wants it! In the 18th century! *God wants it!* These infernal words already opened in the 11th and 12th centuries an abyss in minor Asia to swallow half of Europe there.
In the left of the ribbon one reads these English words; *Will of God!*
The daggers and the sacrileges of the Jesuits are sufficient enough to reveal what can be the God that they cherish! Since their general is their only god, the dagger lying down on the palm leaf is a frightening emblem! It means that one must get, *at any cost*, a sovereign and universal power that can alone assures peace and duration of the order. In case of obstacles to surmount, there is a dagger with the irrefutable order, *God wants it!* It is than that an absolute obedience would make the general *all mighty*!
It is there the great purpose of the Superior Inconnus: but this plan must remain hidden. It is for this reason that most of the symbols are covered with a *new carpet of Masonry*. Instead of the Blazing Star or five-pointed pentagon, the middle of the carpet has a *seven-pointed* star that represents the G and is shaped as a Templar's cross.
Behind the seven-pointed star rise *two eagles*! - The two eagles!
Is there hope to succeed better under the auspices of the *two eagles* rather than *under the shade of the lilies* or under the protection of *the courage of the leopards*?
These two Eagles in 1783 could at the most symbolize the empire! The travels of the Baron of Riesbeck[170] may convince us of the activity of the Jesuits at the court of Vienna. However, we can also see there the hate that the emperor swore to all sects of monks. Therefore, these two eagles of the Scottish carpet only mean the Russian empire, where the Jesuits have in Mogilev a public establishment. The two eagles of the House of Austria and the Russian empire are identified by the various weapons that they carry on their chest. But their chest being covered with the Masonic carpet, the emblem could be understood only by the revelation of the order of the Jesuits, the authors of the allegory.

---

[170] [SE: Baron von Riesbeck. *Travels through Germany*. 1780; tr. by Maty. Dublin 1787. Reprinted 2010 by Nabu Press.]

2. Masonry and Company of Jesus

The rest of the carpet contains only allegories already explained in details in this work: the Masons of our Europe always make the weapon and the shield of the order of the Jesuits there.[171]

Thousands and thousands of other French Degrees are explained as comfortably as the foreign degrees of which I gave the explanation. The *Grand Inspector* G. I. is the General of the Jesuits: the Knights of the Triple Cross[172] – C – are the Jesuit Knights; because three times C, the third letter of the alphabet, give the letter I. In the *Sacrificing* Knights,[173] that is in the order of the Knights of the *society* S., the Member Elect carries the name of Isaac I: it is again our Jerubabel I or Jesuit.

The Knight of the two Eagles[174] is again the Knight of the Jesuits established in Mogilev in Russia. The attribute of this Degree is a nine-pointed star. It is again the letter I: in the middle of the altar is a dagger, it is the dagger of the Jesuits: on the *back* a sun, the emblem of the order, is engraved: the sun is hidden under the back of the medal, because the order of the Jesuits must remain hidden. This degree of the Knight of the Two Eagles mentions that that "the *nine-pointed star* will cause one day in the world as much astonishment and admiration as the view of a phenomenon when it appears in the sky!" The order of the Jesuits, symbolized by the *nine-pointed* star, found suddenly armed by several millions of men, had indeed astonished the universe.

In the Elect *Supreme* Knight[175] we still find the *Ours* of the society. In this degree the ALL-POWERFUL asks how much one worked; one answers him 2186 to obey, 2185 to imitate, and 2184 to perfect. O. I. P. There is first the order of the Jesuit fathers.

First answer: 2 or B; 8 and 1 give the letter I; 6 gives F.

---

[171] The copy of this engraving will appear incessantly with the attachment of the lodge *Réunion des Étrangers* [Meeting of the Strangers].

[172] [SE: In French, *Chevalier de la Triple Croix*. According to Waite, the 66th degree of the collection of the Metropolitan Chapter of France. Also the 20th degree of the Holy Royal Arch Knight Templar Priests]

[173] [SE: *Chevalier Sacrifiant*. According to Waite, Knight of the Sacred Mountain or Knight of Sacrifice, a grade belonging to Masonic Chivalry mentioned in Thory. According to Mackey, a Degree found in the Archives of the Lodge of Saint Louis des Amis Réunis, Saint Louis of the Reunited Friends, at Calais.]

[174] [SE: According to Waite, a grade belonging to Masonic Chivalry mentioned in Thory.]

[175] [SE: *Chevalier Elu Suprême*. 74th grade of the Chapter Metropolitan of France. Also a degree in the collection of Mr. Pyron, and, under the name of Tabernacle of Perfect Elect, is contained in the archives of the Mother Lodge of the Philosophic Rite]

2. Masonry and Company of Jesus

That is B.I.F. *beati Ignatii fratres*, the brethren of the Blissful Ignatius must *obey*: these brethren and servants are the Masons who must *obey* the order. TO OBEY!
Second answer: 2 or B, 8 and 1 give the letter I; 5 gives the *five virtues*.
That is, the brethren must first *obey*; then *imitate* the five virtues ordered by the Blissful Saint Ignatius. TO IMITATE!
Third answer: 2 or B; 8 and 1 give the letter I; 4 the 4 vows of the *Ours*:
That is, the *Ours* of the society must *perfect* the plan thrown by Saint Ignatius or the order of the Blissful Saint Ignatius. TO PERFECT!
All the answers start with the number 2 because it is the *sign* of the Jesuits.

One finds then in the reunion of the three answers, three distinct columns:
TO OBEY: The obedience is the corner stone of the society or the first *column* of the society.

$$\begin{array}{l} 2 \text{ and } 1 \\ 2 \text{ and } 1 \\ \underline{2 \text{ and } 1} \\ 9 \end{array}$$ Or the letter I. Jesuits.

The Jesuits must *obey*.

TO IMITATE! The imitation is the second *column* of the order of the Jesuits.

$$\begin{array}{l} 8 \\ 8 \\ \underline{8} \\ 24 \end{array}$$ *Viginti quatuor seniores*

These are the 24 Elders of whom it is necessary to *imitate* the doctrine and the mental reservations.

TO PERFECT! The last column is the column of *perfection* or of the fathers.

$$\begin{array}{l} 6 \\ 5 \\ \underline{4} \\ 15 \end{array}$$ or O, *ordo*.

It is the order that must *perfect the brethren, the imitators and the fathers.*

The degree of Grand Architect[176] is only composed of Adonhiramite Masonry. A or 1, H or 8; again the numbers 9 or the letter I. The Knights of Saint John, authors of this degree, are nothing but the Knights of Saint Ignatius.

Do we want to see the *Ours* again under another shape?

Let's look for them at the degree of the *Four times Respectable*, Scottish Masters of Saint Andrew of Scotland.[177]

The Four times Respectable are again the *Ours* or the Jesuits, *respectable* by the four vows of the order.

Can we doubt that this degree is not under the domination of the Jesuit priests; the works of the degree begin with the sacrifice of the Holly Mass; and this lodge is held in the Valley of His Highness the Lord Stuart. The degree speaks of the death of *Jacques Ma-Biotte* and assures that the initials express the Master's word. Once again the Jehovah I, the *Mac-Benac* M.B. M. give 12 and B, 2, total 14 or O, *ordo*. *Jacques* gives I. Once again the order of the *Jesuits, ordo Jesuitarum*.

Satis est. I have reached the highest degree of probability on each demonstration; each demonstration is then in conformity with the general history of our Europe. What surprised me, only toward the end of my work, is that I was far from suspecting in France such a great activity among the Jesuits.

It is demonstrated that millions of Masons (the number is approximately twenty millions of them in Europe) are the servile toys of the Jesuits. In the image of the society of their Fathers, they engraved an allegorical tracing board, clear enough to explain the main object of their plots. It is a *child* who *tries to get a foothold on a cloud*, in order to be able to turn the globe of the world over. It includes the following inscription:

Fac pedem figat, et terram movebit. "Give him a place to fix his foot, and he shall move the earth."

---

[176] [SE: A Degree in several of the Rites modeled upon the 12th of the Ancient and Accepted Scottish Rite. It is the 6th Degree of the Reform of Saint Martin; the 14th of the Rite of Elected Cohens; the 23rd of the Rite of Mizraim, and the 24th of the Metropolitan Chapter of France.]

[177] [SE: 4th degree of the present Scottish Rectified Rite (originally an offshoot of Baron von Hund's Rite of Strict Observance)]

2. Masonry and Company of Jesus

[Figure 6 – Fac pedem figat, et terram movebit. *Imago,* **p. 321]**

Would this be insolence and effrontery? D'Alembert probably didn't suspect that his friend David Hume had drawn to the very source of the truth, the idea of the happiest word he had said in his life:

> "The Priests found what Archimedes was looking for, a point in the sky to move the world." [178]

I often spoke in this writing of the Masonic ritual of a supposed late *Samuel Prichard.* The preface of this catechism, for those who don't have the *Jesuitical key*, offers a ridiculous, untrue, contradictory and incomprehensible gibberish. However it includes the copy of a legal act or oath of integrity attesting that all assertions in this Preface are exact and in conformity with the constitutions of the order of the Free and Accepted Masons.

In vain I would have liked to translate this preface; the game of the letters, the double sense and the emphasis of some expressions and some grammatical observations, are insurmountable obstacles, or at least they would require 40 to 50 pages of calculations and tedious details.

Luckily the study of the English language is rather common in France: it is said that the king himself has a perfect knowledge of it.

Reassured by this and by the certainty that this last analysis is absolutely useless to prove the truth of my thesis for a long time demonstrated, I decided to translate only the *spirit* of this preface.

---

[178] [SE: The quote above is an epigraph from the brochure *Des droits du clergé dans les affaires publiques* (1780). The original quote from Hume (*Essays, Moral, Political, and Literary,* Part I, Essay XXI) is "And having got what Archimedes only wanted, (namely, another world, on which he could fix his engines) no wonder they move this world at their pleasure."]

After having analyzed all words, combined the game of the initial letters, and reduced sometimes the letters in numbers and sometimes the numbers in letters, as I made it in all my previous demonstrations, the *deciphered* title of the ritual and the preface gave the following results:

"Generalat.

"The original institution of the papal hierarchy constitutes the foundation of the government of the Universe: but it is in the Generalat of the Jesuits that this universal government is bound today in the strongest manner. The first stone or basis of this government has been laid by the excellent son of the church, Ignatius, who, in his great soul, conceived the plan of the order of the Jesuits and executed it. This plan was followed courageously by the college of Cler'-Mont in Paris. This college soon began to govern the kings of France, and even extended its power in England, where Jacques II, when he was still only duke of York, build in London a public college for the society. It was the custom to receive a Jesuit in the following manner:

One of the elders of the society held the book of the constitutions of the Society of Jesus in front of the one or those who had to swear on the book; and during this ceremony the Master read the constitutions of the order.

According to these constitutions or rules, the Jesuits, without exception, must be faithful to one another; help their brethren and *Ours*: they must rely on them for the administration of the public affairs and must reward them.

But *in these last days*, the order further seized those who *are in no way destined* to share its glory and its enjoyments, unless after have been carefully tested and examined, they are considered capable to become active *Ours*.

This new branch of the order uses the name Free and Accepted Masons instead of Society of Jesus and of the *Ours*: this name of Free and Accepted Mason *is so to speak old*: these lodges and these assemblies held *four* times per year began only since the year 1691, when it was decided to initiate lords, and dukes, jurisconsults, traders, haberdashers, and even doormen, in the secret *that is not a secret*.

The initiates of the first class provide immense sums *to the hidden order*. The other lower classes bring a lot of money; and at least six or seven shillings are collected from the initiates of the last class. In exchange of their money, they are all *given* the apron, which is the attire of the order.[179]

---

[179] It is not a very expensive attire.

2. Masonry and Company of Jesus

They wear it like a badge of honor; they even imagine that this apron is a more honorable distinction than the *star* and *garter*, because they believe, according to the traditions *given* to them, that this apron comes directly from Adam. It is to my dear Coadjutor brethren that I leave to determine how much is founded the belief of the initiates in Masonry.

It is the Jesuit *Ours* who execute today the plan launched by the Blissful Ignatius, first *General* of the order. The new Masons received, for sign of association, the B.I. letters of the college of Cler'-Mount, or *mountain of the clerks* or of the clergy. The new Masons were made aware only of the existence of the fathers of this college.

The general and the order constitute one by the other a society acting *openly and honestly*. *Reliable* men are chosen by the General and by the order to govern the states and they keep a *sacrosanct fidelity*.

As for the initiates in the new Masonry, there is nothing to fear because there is nothing to betray. If someone was not satisfied with this Masonry after his initiation; if he dared to complain that he had been deceived, and that he gave a lot of money for nothing; and if he refuses to pay our common Masonic taxes, it is easy to submit him to obedience; or to get rid of his importunities. *Although received according to all laws of the Masonic constitution*, and while he would satisfy to all signs and grips and catechisms, the entry of the lodges can be closed to him, so that he doesn't have the *hope* anymore to know what he would never have learned from Masons.

It is enough for us that all men who can see realize, while going through the ritual with some intelligence, that everything in it is *premeditated* contradiction."

And then according to his search we will judge if it is necessary to lose him or to seduce him.

This last sentence is not in the original: but it is the necessary consequence of the principles of *Samuel Prichard*.

CONSUMMATUM EST.

"*And the veil of the temple tore in two, from top to bottom.*"

Conclusion

While preparing to take my leave of a respectable society so cruelly abused, I experience the drunkenness the heart feels while taking leave of a dear and beloved friend. We always have something more to say when holding the hand that speaks and that answers. The heart that poured out entirely is still full; but it is a same feeling that fills it chaotically, nothing more can go out of it that is not already in our friend's heart.

I put pen to paper with reluctance, with pain; but it was necessary to raise the voice, for the millions of men seduced and deceived. Friends of innocence, they didn't see the dangers that surrounded them everywhere. I defended our common interests candidly, with all the reflection I could be capable of. I tried more than once to hide from the public those whose untrue writings inspired me with indignation. I tried to draw my proofs only from *anonymous* writers, or in the ranting of some impostors already faded by the public voice. I won't blush of having been admitted in a society of brethren, where I saw so many times the simple and soft virtues being applied in silence: where I saw so many good men, cherish the hope to acquire one day in this society some knowledge for themselves, for their children and for all men!

But what is the real source of this happiness? The Superior Inconnus don't have the slightest part in it. They are not yet in a number great enough, to dare to unveil suddenly the darkness of their intentions. It is enough for them to prepare little by little some partisans, and to give us some mysterious symbols.

The star pentagon of our ancestors has been spoiled; we were beguiled when told the G of the Blazing Star was the greatest secret of the order; and that this important mystery will never be explained to us. Dear God, were those the august mysteries of the priests of nature, who intended so many useful knowledge for us? For about one century, a few millions of men have been played with impunity. Feel with pride, children of nature, that everything that can honor our society, in these modern times, is owed to you solely, and to the sages who enlightened your century; and who alone only prevented that you would already be the victim of the most ridiculous expectations. Have you forgotten the unhappy times of our European crusades, and the Saint-Bartholomew, and the Sicilian Vespers, and the Holy Inquisition, which still stands?

Today we know the principles of these curses on humankind who treated us as slaves. Their doctrine is so awful that murder and ingratitude are justified as soon as they can serve their intentions. I will only mention an example of it. Pope Gregory XIV had declared that assassins were unworthy to enjoy asylums of the church and that they had to be pulled out of them. The 24 elders uphold that there are no assassins but those who received money to kill someone in treason; and that those who kill *only by obligation to their friends* must not be called assassins. This quote from Pascal should encourage you to reread his letters on the morals of the good fathers so that he renders us forever cautious against their scheming and their expectations. The society from which we pull our origin had a certain purpose, a determined purpose, known from all its members. I speak here of these first English Rosicrucians who were faithful to the tenants of Bacon and who met heart and soul to observe and question Nature. What treasure of knowledge would have been inherited by us and by our century if the healthiest philosophy had not been successfully substituted by some projects of vengeance and by the despotism of an association of celibate priests?

Bacon CREATED A NEW WORLD; an invisible world, an earth of blessing. Some priests swore the conquest of it and they are already ready to transform blissful creatures of that world in altered convicts. Should we carry with indifference chains that would be the only inheritance of our children!

The mysterious and dull system, only spoken about in a gloomy manner, will end up deadening our minds; and slaves are always ferocious. To please these beneficent fathers, it is already necessary, at the sad light of a dark lantern, to put a dagger between the hands of one's brother.

What is there therefore in the whole nature that could incite us to become murderers?

Break the dagger of a God-assassin! Break the specter of chains of a monarch altered by blood! May a pure and serene day enlighten us at the temple of nature! Let's go there and warm up under the sun of reason! Let's be human and beneficent! This is the secret of our ancestors, the secret of happiness.

Having given up our Superior Inconnus, let's not lose hope to find the enlightened and generous men who will extend their paternal hands towards us. They are rare; but great men are rare in every century and yet every century had great men. Those won't hide from us, they won't be our Superiors. They will be our brethren. And to know their merit will be enough for us to follow their advice and to honor them as our fathers. They will teach us to find back the Almighty in the immensity of the creation. They will teach us to know *ourselves* and to respect ourselves and liked others, as beings intended to be born as gods.

It is true that we don't have a system of Masonic knowledge arrived from Adam until our days by an uninterrupted chain of enlightened brethren. However we find in every century and among nearly all civilized peoples some societies of sages that can serve, at least partially, as models to ours.

In all ages, good people met through a brotherly relationship. Enemies of tyranny, and fearing persecution, they hid their assemblies from the vulgar eyes. It was the happy family pleasantly portrayed by the author of the *Système Social*. I am convinced that most of these societies, according to the customs and the mind of their centuries, cannot escape a number of imperfections. However, due to some mistakes that pertain to human nature, it would be unfair to despise a society whose main object was the happiness of its fellows and whose leaders never lost sight from a general perfection.

The Genesis mentions that the descendants of Seth, almost at the time of the birth of the arts, formed between them a chosen society, separated from the rest of people abandoned to all crimes. If it is true, as stated by history, that they promised faith and fraternity under the shadow of Adam, one could joke comfortably as Voltaire did of their devout simplicity. However, Moses, the great Legislator of a people of slaves whose chains he broke, distinguished these children of Seth from all others men. And to render justice for their courageous efforts, he calls them *children of God* and called their contemporaries the *children of men*. The Brahmins have always devoted themselves to the study of nature. This was their religious mysteries and they hid its interpretation and use from the multitude. Like the Eternal, they worked for the happiness of men with an invisible hand. Their courage to defend and to honor their homeland make them still today respectable to the friends of humanity. The Magi, in the presence of their dedicated fire, had to be quite dear to the Persians whose youth they instructed. They taught virtue like a science, necessary for health, happiness, and glory of the homeland. They spoke about cherishing virtue in a beloved wife and in the joys of paternal love. They incited hate for vice, which imposes all these awful and visible curses on its victims. To them, to speak to people about the reward or the punishment of a celestial *avenger* or *remunerator* would have been to damage the courage and the merit of beautiful actions. We can make mistakes but we should not be despised for giving considerable thought on human nature. At the hour of his defeat, Varro was honored by the Romans for not having despaired about the republic. The Egyptians made a mystery of all their natural knowledge. They feared the concern of an idle people in a fertile region. One would have had every day to endure the *wounds* and *curses* almost as terrible as those of Moses. As for the druids, some serious authors draw frightening pictures of their government. However, Tacit and Montesquieu, these two great writers who didn't bring to a century of darkness the customs and ideas that were not there, seize us with a religious terror that creates respect by telling us about these sovereign priests who made both German and Scandinavians the most ferocious people at war and the most human ones at home. Hume, maybe the wisest and most enlightened modern historian, found that only the ferocity of the druids in England could contain the impatience and the harshness of the ancients Bretons, as cruel as they were stupid.[180]

---

[180] David Hume. History of England. Vol. I, p. 4. "Thus the bands of government, Which were generally loose amongst that rough and turbulent People, Were *happily* Corroborated by the terrors of their Superstition."
In a *History of the Modern Europe*, one will find greater details on the customs of the Druids and Germans, *Germani*, People of brethren. (Probably *History of the modern Europe*: since the irruption of the peoples of the North in the empire Roman, until the peace of 1783, 3 vol. Paris; Geneva, [s.n.], 1789-1792.).

2. Masonry and Company of Jesus

These unfortunate Gnostics were ashamed of celibacy. They thought that to honor the eternal more worthily in their temples could only be accomplished by a respectful study of the mysteries of the creation and the miracles of nature. So, the heart is torn, when we see tyranny hunt them with sword and fire.

If we had to blame the Templars only for the religious dogmas brought from the Orient from these priests of the nature, and if they had lived in a century as enlightened as ours, it is likely that our history would not be tarnished by so many abominable cruelties.

I don't believe that it is easy to prove an immediate relationship between the disciples of Bacon and all the particular societies I have just spoken about. However, some traces of it could certainly be found in all societies of Sages of the ancient world. This is because, *within the meaning of the new Atlantis* of Bacon, anyone having a tendency to study Nature would be found to be altogether Brahmin, Magus, Druid, Gnostic, Templar, Rosicrucian, and always Christian.

Therefore, let's purify the temple of Nature. And may our august symbols, soiled by bloodthirsty monks, stop being an object of disgust and fright for the sages. They are worth being studied.

Voltaire wrote that the mysteries of Freemasons were quite dull.[181] This writer never wanted to believe that something could escape his insight, or at least he tried to convince the Universe that it was so.

The vanity of wanting to explain everything at a glimpse led him to commit an action unworthy of him and of all good man. I tend to believe that nature and time took back great secrets from indifferent men; but it is not wise to treat with great contempt the symbols that were cherished by so many great men. We can easily forgive a dry joke made by this great writer. His writings are full of light self-contradictions. He indulged without restrains in the diversity of his ideas that passions shifts so easily. His talents were precious and infinitely rarer than those of J.J. and of Condorcet. However, did he have the heart of Jean Jacques? Did he have the mind of Condorcet? It seems that he only had a side view of objects, that he only saw them through a prism of one thousand colors that turns them upside down and disfigures them. We owe him eternal homage for having fought all his life an insane fanaticism born from voluntary ignorance, that does not look for the reason of things, that takes everything for prodigies, that sinks into mistakes and thinks of authorizing crimes by a great number of accomplices. He pursued, under all its shapes, the ferocious guilty person who wanted to escape remorse by hastily making believed what he believed without reflection. But mainly focused on gathering with skills *acquired* ideas, he did not focus his thoughts on a future that has not happened yet. I think this is why he has more tricks in the style than inventions in the ideas.

---

[181] *Questions sur l'Encyclopédie*, chapter on *Initiation*. [SE: Volume 6 (1779), p. 43. "Ces mystères sont bien plats, mais on ne se parjure presque jamais."]

There is a certain elegance in the style, said Jean Jacques, that it is not difficult to give to little things. Montaigne, an irrefutable judge in the matter of style, didn't want the *dexterity of the hand* as much as the merriment of the imagination that elevates and fills a language of the heart. He did not want words *of wind*; he wanted *words of flesh and bone*, words that bring *weight* and *density* to their signification.

> "Gallus speaks simply because he conceives simply. Horace does not content himself with a superficial expression; that would betray him; he sees farther and more clearly into things; his mind breaks into and rummages all the magazine of words and figures wherewith *to express himself*, and he must have them more than ordinary because his conception is so."[182]

So, there is an immense interval between Voltaire, who handled with a treacherous charm the arms of ridicule, cruel present of nature; and Bacon, who prepared and calculated treasures reserved to his last nephews! Who, through trials and new combinations, wanted to push nature to the end, and to pull its veil and its secrets. He believed it is often possible to discover the reasons by the extremes, like the strength of iron and stones in the liquids and light by darkness. He implored the Sages to meet armed with their experience. With the enthusiasm of a genius that hints to the true Prophet of the Eternity, he assured them that if they questioned Matter every day so that it could speak to them, they would comprehend in the universal science of the shapes, the initial, elementary and indestructible principle that would put all the operations of nature between their creative hands.

---

[182] Montaigne. *Essays*. Book 3, chap. 4.

2. Masonry and Company of Jesus

3. Masonry Dissected

with Notes and Proofs

Introduction

The work titled *Masonry Dissected* is extremely rare today but more than twenty editions exist. While I hold in my hands the twenty-first one and it is unlikely that it is the last one.

In all Masonic works published for the last twenty years, it has never been cited. I found only one writer who mentioned it as a *rather extraordinary* book. Now, this writer is certainly not the slave of the Unknown Superiors. and I cannot convince myself that today he his the only one in Europe who knows the Catechism of the said deceased *Samuel Prichard*. On the contrary, I believe that the two or three thousands Jesuits who wrote about Masonry in England, in Germany, in Italy and in France know him quite well; but attempts are made to forget about him, after trying everything to eliminate the prints exposed by public sales.

This *Masonry Dissected* contains the most ancient ritual of Masonic lodges in England. The purpose of the Jesuits is found much less veiled in it than in all other works. By itself, it can prove the *alteration* of the principles and rites of the Society of Masons for which the honest and sacrosanct observance, so much bragged about by Mr. Smith and all, is a chimera if not a bold assertion. I felt necessary to add to my work an exact copy of the English text. It was difficult for me to acquire a copy and I have not doubts that this new edition will be precious for many Masons. This Ritual not only confirms all strange things that were said in our research but it will serve as a *universal key* for all other writings about French Masonry by Jesuits.

3. Masonry Dissected – Notes and Proofs

MASONRY DISSECTED

BEING AN
UNIVERSAL AND GENUINE
DESCRIPTION
Of
All its BRANCHES, from the ORIGINAL
to the PRESENT TIME:
As it is delivered in the
Constituted Regular Lodges,
Both in CITY and COUNTRY,
According to the
Several DEGREES of ADMISSIONS.

Giving an impartial Account of their Regular Proceedings
in initiating their NeW Members in the Whole Three
Degrees of FREE MASONRY;

VIZ,

I. ENTER'D PRENTICE.   II. FELLOW-CRAFT.
III. MASTER

With
A new and exact LIST of REGULAR LODGES,
According to their Seniority and Constitution.

By SAMUEL PRICHARD,
Late Member of a CONSTITUTED LODGE,

To Which is added,

The AUTHOR'S VINDICATION of Himself:

Together With the Copy of the OATH that he took before
an Alderman, that this Was a true Copy of FREE-MASONRY.

The Twenti-First Edition.

LONDON,

Printed for Byfield and Hawkesworth, the
Corner of Craig's-Court, Charing-Crofs
(Price Six-Pence.)

3. Masonry Dissected – Notes and Proofs

Samuel Prichard Maketh Oath,
     That the Copy hereunto annexed,
     is a True and Genuine Copy in every Particular.
Jur° 13 *die oct.*
1730, *coram me*   *Samuel Prichard*
R. Hopkins.

Bonneville's Notes on the Title

To facilitate the reading of the code of this ritual, we include here some observations that could be missed, even by attentive readers, because of the peculiarity of the *monastic game* adopted by Jesuits.

About the title Masonry *Dissected.* D and M give the numbers 4 and 12. These three numbers then give the number 7 or the letter G, General.
Nothing harder and forceful than the title *Masonry Dissected*: In our language, *Dissected Masonry* cannot me more barbarian as a title. However, the title was meant to indicate the Generalate of the Jesuits. In addition, to indicate here that it is about the *Generalate* and not the General symbolized by the emblematic G, the title announces a stripping down of the G *in all its branches from its origin to today*: it is therefore about the history of the *Generalate* written from the origin of the Society of St. Ignatius up of the conquest of Masonry. This is why we find in the sixth line of the title: "All its BRANCHES from the Original to the present time."

Constituted regular lodges C.R.L., which is to say 3, 17, and 11. These make 31. These two numbers 3 and 1 give 4, and represent the Professed of the four Vows or the *Our*.
If luck alone caused such result, only gibberish would be found in these words of the title: *As is it delivered in the constituted regular lodges.*
This line of the title means: Here is the history of the Generalate of the order, *such as the Nostri have given it to the lodges regularly constituted by them.*
If the meaning I discover in this assertion was not that of Samuel Prichard, he would have only said a lie; because no Mason has ever received the explanation *in the lodge* of *all the branches of Masonry*, from its origin to nowadays. On the contrary, one does not tire inventing the most stupid and all-monastic allegories to dissipate the core idea of Bacon of Verulam, who wanted to create a *literary society*. He even gave this title to his Atlantis.

3. Masonry Dissected – Notes and Proofs

A new proof that Samuel Prichard did not want to make a lie that could be found by all Masons is that he placed on the back of the title page a *legal attestation*, to state that he said the truth.

The Editor of *Dissected Masonry* attributes the Book to a said *deceased* Samuel Prichard, herein *late member* of a CONSTITUED LODGE C 3 L 11.

Three and Eleven give 14 or *ordo.* It was meant therefore that *Samuel Prichard* was once a member of the Jesuit Order. If he were not initiated in the Order, would he have been capable to write the preliminary discourse; he would have never been able to legally attest that his *Dissected Masonry* was "A true and genuine Copy in *every particular.*"

Dedication

To The

Rt. Worshipful and Honourable

Fraternity

Of

Free and Accepted Masons

Brethren and Fellows,

If the following Sheets, done without Partiality, gain the universal Applause of so worthy a Society, I doubt not but their general Character will be diffused and esteemed among the remaining Polite Part of Man-Kind' Which, I hope will give entire Satisfaction to all Lovers of Truth; and I shall remain, with all humble Submission, the Fraternity's

Most Obedient

Humber Servant,

SAM. PRICHARD

3. Masonry Dissected – Notes and Proofs

Masonry Dissected

THE original Institution of Masonry consisted in the Foundation of the Liberal Arts and Sciences, but more especially on the Fifth, viz *Geometry*. For, at the Building of the Tower of *Babel*, the Art and Mystery of Masonry was first introduced, and from thence handed down by *Euclid*, a worthy and excellent Mathematician of the *Egyptians*, and he communicated it to *Hiram*, the Master Mason concerned in the Building of *Solomon's* Temple in *Jerusalem*; where was an excellent and curious Mason that was the Chief under the Grand-Master Hiram, whole Name was *Mannon Grecus*; who taught the Art of Masonry to one *Carolus Marcel*, in France; who was afterwards elected King of *France*; and from thence was brought into *England* in the Time of King *Athelstan*, who ordered an Assembly to be held once every Year at *York*; which was the first Introduction of it into *England*, and Masons were made in the Manner following.

Tunc unus ex Senioribus teneat Librum, ut ille vel illi ponat vel ponant Manus supra Librum; dum precepta debeant legi: i.e. Whilst one of the Seniors holdeth the Book, that he or they put their hands upon the Book, whilst the Master ought to read the Laws or Charges.

Which Charges were, That they should be true to one another without Exception, and should be obliged to relieve their Brothers and Fellows Necessities, or put them to Labour, and reward them accordingly.

But in these latter Days, Masonry is not composed of Artificers, as it was in its primeval State, when some few Catechetical Questions were necessary to declare a Man sufficiently qualified for an operative Mason. The Term of Free and Accepted Masonry [as it now is] has not been heard of till within these few Years: No constituted lodges or Quarterly Communications were heard of till 1691, when Lords and Dukes, Lawyers and Shopkeepers, and other inferior Tradesmen, Porters not excepted, were admitted into this Mystery, or no Mystery. The first Sort-being introduced at a very great Expense, the second Sort at a moderate Rate, and the latter for the Expense of six or seven Shillings, for which they receive that Badge of Honour, which [as they term it] is more ancient and more honourable than is the Star and Garter; which Antiquity is accounted, according to the Rules of Masonry, as delivered by their Tradition, ever since *Adam*, which I shall leave to the candid Reader to determine.

From the Accepted Masons sprang the Real Masons, from both sprang the *Gormogons*, whose Grand-Master the *Volgi* deduces his Original from the

Chinese, whose Writings, if to be credited, maintained the *Hypothesis* of the *Pre-Adamites*, and consequently, must be more antique than Masonry.

The most free and open Society is that of the *Grand Kaibeber* which consists of a select Company of responsible People, whose chief Discourse is concerning Trade and Business; and promoting mutual Friendship, without Compulsion or Restriction.

But after the Admission into the Secrets of Masonry, if any new Brother should dislike their proceedings, and reflect upon himself; for being so easily cajoled out of his Money, declining the Fraternity, or secluding himself upon the Account of the Quarterly Expense of the lodge, and Quarterly Communications, notwithstanding he has been legally admitted into a constituted and regular lodge, he shall be denied the privilege [as a Visiting Brother] of knowing the Mystery, for which he has already paid: Which is a manifest Contradiction, according to the Institution of Masonry itself, as will evidently appear by the Following Treatise.

Bonneville's Notes on the Preliminary Discourse

This preliminary discourse seems to offer only ridicule and unintelligible assertions; however, this is where "the letter kills, but the spirit gives life."[183] The introduction of this catechism is done with a subtlety that one could merely think possible, because ingenious and skillful combinations were necessary to hide symbolically in it the true origin of the power of Jesuits in Masonry.

By comparing the universal history with the hidden meaning under some multiplied numbers, we will learn that the primitive institution covered here can only relate to the intrigues of the popes who solely occupy themselves with the study of the *art and science* of subjugating Kings and Empires. And to express that this politics was still subjected to the politics of the Jesuits,

---

[183] [SE: 2 Corinthians 3:6]

Samuel Prichard says that in the 16th century, the foundations of the *geometric Science*, G. S. were being established. In other words, the All Mightiness of the General of the Society of the Jesuits *Generalis Societatis* was under preparation in the 16th century.

The time of this establishment needed to stay hidden, it is found symbolized by the word BABEL, B2, A1, B2, E5, L11; these numbers 2, 1, 2, 5, 11 give the number 21; 15 is omitted from it, to express by abbreviation the year 1521; and this is the date of the famous pilgrimage of Ignatius of Loyola. It was then that he contemplating the plan of his order that would subject Kings and People to its power.

The name of this famous General is symbolized by the name EUCLID; E5, U20, C3, L11, I19, D4; all these numbers give 52. These last two numbers 5 and 2 give 7 or the letter G. which always signifies the General of the Order.

The General is called a worthy and excellent mathematician of the *Egyptians*, to have the initial E, which is to say allegorically the church. *Egyptians* is found in the plural to have for total a number 9 or the letter I, which is to say the *Jesuit church*.

Samuel Prichard wanted to express by his symbol that S. Ignatius left the *church*, which is to say the fundamental point of the politics of the popes to become himself a Hiram or a new architect who builds a new building. This new building represents Salomon temple in Jerusalem. The two words *Salomon* and *Jerusalem* are printed in italic letters to show that they are the only important words. These two words *Salomon* and *Jerusalem* specifically express, through their initial letters S. J., the Society of the Jesuits.

Mannon Grecus taught the art of Masonry to a certain *Charles Martel* who was then elected King of France. In the 15th and 16th centuries, there was no *Charles Martel* King of France. It is therefore not what was meant to be expressed: A C and a M were needed to symbolize the college of Clermont, C. M. This college of Clermont, or mount of the clergy, represents the Order of the Jesuits. This Charles Martel, who was elected king of France, allegorically means that the Jesuits succeeded in governing the kings of France. The *Mannon Grecus,* or general of the Perfect Initiates, expresses all the means used to firmly establish the college of Clermont.

It is from France that the order was moved to England. We explained earlier that King Athelston and the assemblies of York specifically refer to King Jacques II who established in London a College of Jesuits when he was Duke of York.

Laws or charges. These laws or charges represent the Book of Constitutions of the Society of Jesus, which is, so to speak, the book of the order. And to avoid confusion the two initials of these words laws and charges, L 11 and C 3, give the number 14, which is to say the letter O.

"Their Brothers and Fellows Necessities." This sentence requires an attentive analysis, especially in French; because one should not translate it by *les nécessités ou besoins de leurs frères et compagnons.* In English, it should be written: "Their Brothers and Fellows' Necessities": *Necessities* is found here for a name of sect or of particulars.

Now what sect is it? The sect of *necessities* is a blunder. However, this word symbolizes the *Our* because the term *necessities* gives the initial of *Nostri*.

Then all is clear, all complies with the rules of the discourse: "One must help the *Nostri* brothers." This is the idea of Samuel Prichard.

Samuel Prichard could not make the lineage of Masonry come straight from Adam up to today, but he dares not contradict those who stated it. He is rather generous to leave the discussion of this historical feature to the *candid* reader – C –, which is to say the *coadjutor*, because here we enter in the Order of the Jesuits and learn about the power of the order over Masonry.

Samuel Prichard express the Society of the Jesuits by the words *Free-Masons* – F 6, M 12, or 6 and 12 give 18 or the letter S. *societas*. This is to say that they are the disciples of Saint Ignatius, who calls them *Real-Masons* R 17, M 12: now 17 and 12 give 29. The numbers 2 and 9 then give the letters B. I. Beatus Ignatius; he then calls them *Accepted* Masons, to symbolize the *Our* A 1, M 12. The numbers 12 and 1 give 13 or the letter N *Nostri.*

In this introduction the Free-Masons are still called *Gormongons* to have a number 9 or the letter I. This word of *nine letters* begins by the letter G, because the Masons *have nothing to see* in the loges but the G that spoils the Pythagorean pentagon.

He still calls the Masons *Volgi*, V 21, 2 and 1 make 3; in this way the initial of *Volgi* symbolizes the initial of *Vota* and the numbers give the number 3 to express the three vows or the three grades of the Masonry of Samuel Prichard.

He adds that these Volgi draw their origin from the Chinese – C – This letter symbolizes again the college of Cler'-mont that establishes in England a Masonry composed of three Jesuit degrees or professions.

"Whose Writings if to be credited, maintained the hypothesis of *Pre-Adamics*, and consequently must be more antique than Masonry." Our public history clarifies this rodomontade even more: it is true that the fathers of the College of Cler'-mont are older than their Masonic establishments. In this way their secret history is right to call them *Pre-Adamites* P.A. or *patres anteriores*, some *fathers anterior* to *contemporary* Masonry that, without them, would never have received symbols of horror and ridicule hopes.

The Great *Kai-Be-Ber* symbolizes at the same time the *general* and the *order*. Great G, is the general: the initials of the *three* syllables of the name Kai-Be-Ber – K 10, B 2, B 2 – give the number 14 or the letter O, *ordo*. The Great Kai-Be-Ber is therefore the *general of the order*.

He even proceeds to explain the kind of work done in the society of the *Great Kai-Be-Ber* by all intrepid and *hardworking* man. This elected society, of *responsible people* R.P. or *reverendorum patrum*, focuses specifically on *public affairs, commerce, negotiation, administration*, and so forth.

"Their *chief* discourse is Trade and Business."
The name *responsible people* given by him to the reverent Jesuit fathers is an impertinence that one cannot suspect, unless being well-versed in the spirit of the English language: Lord Chatham would be called a responsible man when he is Minister of England, but such name would rarely be given to any foreign power by an Englishman.

Based on these observations and on the other Jesuit codes already explained so many times, any reader who has no knowledge about Masonry, if he knows English, should be able to read to preface to the ritual as I translated it.

Enter'd Prentice's Degree

Q. From whence came you?
A. From the Holy lodge of St. *John's*.
Q. What Recommendations brought you from thence?
A. The Recommendation which I brought from the Right Worshipful Brothers and Fellows[184] of the Right worshipful and Holy lodge of *St. John's*; from whence I came, and greet you thrice heartily well.
Q. What do you come here to do?
A. Not to do my own proper will,[185]
　　But to subdue my Passion still;
　　The Rules of Masonry in Hand to take;
　　And daily Progress therein to make.
Q. Are you a Mason?
A. I am so taked and accepted to be amongst Brothers and Fellows.[186]
Q. How shall I know that you are a Mason?
A. By Signs and Tokens, and perfect Points of my Entrance.
Q. What are Signs?
A. All Squares, Angles, and Perpendiculars.
Q. What are Tokens?
A. Certain Regular and Brotherly Gripes.

Exam. Give me the first, and I will give you the second.
Exam. I hail it.
Resp. I conceal it.
Exam. What do you conceal?
Resp. All Secrets and Secrecy of Mans and Masonry,[187] unless to a True and lawful Brother, after due Examination, or in a just and worshipful Lodge of Brothers and Fellows well met.

Q. Where was you made a Mason?

---

[184] Brothers and Fellows – *Scholastici et coadjutores spirituales*; because the temporal Jesuits are still not part of the Order. Their church and the Ours must remain unknown.
[185] Proper will – Because the order of the Jesuits requires an absolute obedience.
[186] Amongst Brothers and Fellows – Because the temporal Jesuits do not know yet that Masonry is within the hands of the Society of Jesus.
[187] Secrets and secrecy of *Masons* – Secret of the Ours.

A. In a just and perfect Lodge.
Q. What makes a just and perfect Lodge?
A. Seven or more.
Q. What do they consist of?
A. One Master, two Wardens, two Fellow-Crafts, and two Enter'd Prentices.
Q. What makes, a Lodge?
A. Five.
Q. What do they consist of?
A. One Master, two Wardens, one Fellow Craft, and one enter'd' Prentice.
Q. How did he bring you?
A. Neither naked nor cloathed, bare-foot nor shod, deprived of all Metal, and in a right moving Posture.
Q. How got you Admittance?
A. By three great Knocks.
Q. Who received you?
A. A Junior Warden.
Q. How did he dispose of you?
A. He carried me up to the North-east Part of the lodge, and brought me back again to the West and delivered me to the Senior Warden.
Q. What did the Senior Warden do with you?
A. He presented me, and showed me how to walk up [by three Steps] to the Master.
Q. What did the Master do with you?
A. He made me a Mason.
Q. How did he make you a Mason?
A. With my bare banded Knee and Body within the Square, the Compass extended to my naked Left Breast, my naked Right Hand on the Holy Bible: There I took the Obligation [or Oath of a Mason.]
Q. Can you repeat that Obligation?
A. I'll do my Endeavour. [*Which is as follows:*]

I Hereby solemnly Vow and Swear, in the Presence of Almighty God, and this Right Worshipful Assembly; that I will Hail and conceal, and never Reveal the Secrets or Secrecy of Mason or Masonry, that shall be revealed unto me; unless to a True, and Worshipful lodge of Brothers and Fellows well met.

I furthermore Promise and Vow, that I will not Write them, Print them, Mark them, Carve them, or Engrave them, on Wood or Stone, so as the Visible Character or Impression of a Letter may appear, whereby it may be unlawfully obtained.

All this under no less Penalty, than to have my Throat cut, my Tongue taken from the Roof of my Mouth, my Heart plucked from under my Left Breast; then to be buried in the Sand of the Sea, the Length of a Cable Rope front

3. Masonry Dissected – Notes and Proofs

Shore, where the Tide ebbs and flows twice in twenty-four Hours; my Body to be burnt to Ashes, my Ashes to be scattered upon the Face of the Earth, so that there shall be no more Remembrance of me among Masons.

So help me God.

Q. What Form is the lodge
A. A long Square.
Q. How long?[188]
Q. How broad?
A. Front North to South.
Q. How high?
A. Inches, Feet and Yards innumerable, as high as the Heavens.
Q. How deep?
A. To the Centre of the Earth.
Q. Where does the lodge sland?
A. Upon holy Ground, or the highest Hill or lowest Vale, or in the Vale of *Jehosaphat,*[189] or any other secret Place.
Q..How is it situated?
A. Due East and West
Q. Why so?
A.. Because all Churches and Chapels[190] are, or ought to be so.
Q. What supports a lodge?
A. Three great Pillars.[191]
Q. What are they called?
A. Wisdom, Strength and Beauty:
Q. Why so?
A. Wisdom to contrive, Strength to support, and Beauty to adorn.
Q. What Covering have you to the lodge?
A. A cloudy Canopy of divers Colours [or the Clouds.]
Q. Have you any Furniture in your lodge?
A. Yes.
Q. What is it?
A. *Mosaick* Pavement,[192] Blazing Star,[193] and Indented Tarsel.

---

[188] How Long? – the answer is omitted in the text.
[189] Vale of Jehosaphat J – The Jesuits: in other words the entire surface of the globe, where Masons must not know that they are the slaves of Jesuits.
[190] Churches and Chapels – Because the lodges represent churches.
[191] Three great Pillars – The three Vows.
[192] Furniture, *Mosaick* Pavement – Mosaick is written in the text in italic letters to symbolize the artifice used by Moses to blind the Israelites and make partisans of them.
[193] Blazing Star – The Blazing Star, or sun, is the emblem of the order, the symbol of the Almighty. This is why we find here this almighty G, which hides the General.

Q. What are they?

A. *Mosaick* Pavement for the Ground-floor of the lodge, Blazing Star the Centre, and indented Tarsel the Border round about it.

Q. What is the other Furniture of a lodge?

A. A Bible, Compass and Square.

Q. Who do they properly belong to?

A. A Bible to God, Compass to the Master, and Square to the Fellow-Craft.

Q: Have you any Jewels in your lodge?

A Yes.

Q. How many?

A. Six, three moveable, and three immoveable.

Q. What are the moveable Jewels?

A. Square, Level, and Plumb-Rule.

Q. What are their Uses?

A. Square to lay down true and right Lines, Level to try all Horizontals, and the Plumb-rule to try all Uprights.

Q. What are the immoveable Jewels?

A. Tarsel Board, Rough Ashler, and Broached Thurnel.

Q. What are their Uses?

A. A Tarsel Board for the Master to draw his Designs upon, Rough ashler for the Fellow-craft to try their Jewels upon, and the Enter'd Prentice to learn to work upon.

Q. Have you any Lights in your lodge?

A. Yes, three.

Q. What do they represent?

A. Sun, Moon, and Master Mason.[194]

N. B. These Lights are three large Candles placed on high Candlesticks.

Q. Why so?

A. Sun to rule the Day, Moon, the Night, and Master Mason his lodge.

Q. Have you any fixed Lights in your lodge?

A. Yes,

Q. How many?

A. Three.

N.B. These fixed Lights are three Windows,[195] supposed [though vainly] to be in every Room Where a lodge is held; but more properly the four Cardinal Points according to the antique Rules of Masonry.

Q. How are they situated?

A. East, South, and West.

---

[194] Sun, moon and *Master Mason* – The master of the Masons or of the Ours. Once more, it is the general.

[195] Windows. – See page 99 and page 104.

3. Masonry Dissected – Notes and Proofs

Q. What are their Uses?
A. To light the Men to, and from their Work.
Q. Why are there no Lights in the North?
A. Because the Sun darts no Rays from thence.
Q. Where stands your Master?
A. In the East
Q. Why so?
A. As the Sun rises in the East and opens the Day, so the Master stands in the East [*With his Right Hand upon his Left Breast, being a Sign, and the Square about his Neck*] to open the lodge, and to set his Men at work.
Q. Where Stands your Wardens?
A. In the West.
Q. What's their Business?
A. As the Sun sets in the West to close the Day, so the Wardens stand in the West [*With their Right-Hands upon their Left Breast, being a Sign, and the Level, and Plumb-Rule about their Neck*] to close the lodge, and dismiss the Men from Labour, paying them their Wages.
Q. Where stands the Senior Enter'd Prentice?
A. In the South.
Q. What is his Business?
A. To hear and receive Intructions, and welcome strange Brothers.
Q. Where stands the Junior Enter'd 'Prentice?
A. In the North.
Q. What is his Business?
A. To keep out all Cowans and Evesdroppers.
Q. If a Cowan [or Listner] is catched, how is he to be punished?
A. To be placed under the Eves of the House [in rainy Weather] till the Water runs in at his Shoulders, and out at his Shoulders, and out at his Shoes.
Q. What are the Secrets of a Mason?
A. Signs, Tokens, and many Words.
Q. Where do you keep these secrets?
A. Under my Left Breast.
Q. Have you any Key to those Secrets?
A. Yes.
Q. Where do you keep it?
A,. In a bone Box, that neither opens nor shuts but with ivory keys.
Q. Does it hang, or does it lie?
A. It hangs.
Q. What does it hang by?
A. A Tow Line nine Inches or ar Span.
Q. What Metal is it of?
A. No manner of Metal at all; but a Tongue of good Report is as good behind a brother's Back as before his Face.

N. B. The Key is the Tongue, the Bone-Box the Teeth, the Tow-Line the Roof of the Mouth.

Q. How many Principles are there in Masonry?
A. Four.[196]
Q. What are they?
A. Point, Line, Superficies, and Solid.
Q. Explain them
A. Point the Centre [*round which the Master cannot err*] Line, Length without Breadth; Breadth, Superficies, Length and Breadth; Solid comprehends the Whole.
Q. How many principal Signs?
A. Four.
Q. What are they?
A. Guttural, Pectoral, Manual, and Pedestal.
Q. Explain them?
A. Guttural the Throat; Pectoral the Breast; Manual the Hand; Pedestal the Feet.
Q. What do you learn by being a Gentleman-Mason?
A. Secrecy, Morality, and good Fellowship.
Q. What do you learn by being an Operative-Mason?
A. Hue, Square, Mouldstone, lay a Level and raise a Perpendicular.
Q. Have you seen your Master To-day.?
A. Yes.
Q. How was he cloathed?
A. In a yellow Jacket, and blue Pair of Breeches.

N. B. The yellow Jacket is the Compasses, and the blue Breeches the Steel Points..

Q. How long do you serve your Master?
A. From *Monday* Morning to *Saturday* Night.[197]
Q. How do you serve him?
A. With Chalk, Charcoal, and Earthen Pan.
Q. What do they denote?
A. Freedom, Fervency, and Zeal.[198]

Examp. Give me the Enter'd Prentice's Sign.
Resp. Extending the Four Fingers of the Right hand, and drawing of them cross his Throat, is the Sign, and demands a Token.

---

[196] Four principles – The four vows of the Ours.
[197] From Monday Morning till Saturday night – Sunday is taken of to indicate that the Jesuits intended their slaves for warring works.
[198] Freedom, Fervency and Zeal – F. F. Z. or 6, 6, 24, which give 36, the numbers 3 and 6 give the number 9 or the letter I. The catechism signifies that Freemasons can only be the slaves of the Jesuits.

3. Masonry Dissected – Notes and Proofs

N.B. *A Token is by joining the Ball of the Thumb of the Right Hand upon the First Knuckle of the Forefinger of the Brother's Right-Hand; that demands a Word.*

Q. Give me the Word?
A. I'll letter it with you.

Exam. BOAZ. [N.B. *Exam.* says B. *Resp.* O. *Exam.* A. *Resp.* Z. i. e. Boaz] Give me another.
Resp. JACHIN. [N.B. Boaz *and* Jachim *were two* Pillars in Solomon's *Porch*; I Kings, Chap. vii. Ver. 21.][199]

Q. How old are you?
A. Under Seven.[200] *[Denoting he had not passed Master.]*
Q. What's the Day[201] for?
A. To see in.
Q. What's the Night[202] for?
A. To hear.
Q. How blows the Wind?
A. Due East and West.
Q. What's o'clock?
A. High Twelve.

The End of the Enter'd Prentice's Part.

---

[199] Boaz, Jachin – Here B is found before I. The allegory is quite apparent and was quickly veiled.
[200] Under Seven – This expresses the idea that apprentice Masons are not yet priests since they have not yet received the seven ecclesiastic ordainments. Later, several other Masonic systems say *three years and more* to express the four vows of the Ours.
[201] Day – The flame of the world, or sun, the Order of the Jesuits.
[202] Night – The flame of the nights, or moon, the Order of Freemasons.

Fellow-Craft's Degree

Q: Are you a Fellow-Craft?
A. I am.
Q. Why was you made a Fellow-Craft?
A. For the Sake of the Letter G.[203]
Q. What does that G denote?
A. Geometry, or the fifth Science.[204]
Q. Did you ever travel?
A. Yes, East and West.
Q. Did you ever work?
A. Yes, in the Building of the Temple.
Q. Where did you receive your Wages?
A. In the Middle Chamber.[205]
Q. How came you to the Middle Chamber?
A. Through the Porch.
Q. When you came through the Porch, what did you see?
A. Two great Pillars.
Q. What are they called?
A. J. B. i.e. *Jachin* and *Boaz*.
Q. How high are they?
A. Eighteen Cubits.
Q. How much in Circumference?
Pt. Twelve Cubits.
Q. What were they adorn'd with
A. Two Chapiters.
Q- How high were the Chapters?
A. Five Cubits.
Q. What were they adorn'd with?

Vide I Kings, Chapt. 7.

---

[203] For the sake of the letter G – The unique purpose suggested here is to have the Freemasons blindly obey the General of the Jesuits.

[204] Geometry or fifth Science – It is the art and science of the G, it is the art of subjugating popes, kings and empires.

[205] Middle Chamber – M 12, C 3, giving the number 15 or the letter P, patres. In the past, the priests used to eat the sacrificial meat *in media camera* or in the *middle chamber*. These patres or P are also the portico through which the contemporary Masons enter into their society; having established the contemporary Masonry, they have called themselves allegorically the portico of Masonry.

3. Masonry Dissected – Notes and Proofs

A. Net-work and Pomegranates |
Q. How came you to the Middle Chamber?
A. By a winding Pair of Stairs.[206]
Q. How many?
A. Seven or more.
Q. Why seven or more?
A. Because seven or more make a just and perfect lodge.
Q. When you came to the Door of the Middle-Chamber, who did you see?
A. A Warden.
Q. what did he demand of you?
A. Three Things.[207]
Q. What were they?
A. Sign, Token, and a word.

N. B. *The Sign is placing the Right Hand on the Left Breast; the Token is by joining your Right Hand to the Person that demands it; and squeezing him with the Ball of your Thumb on the first Knuckle of the Middle Fingers and the Word is Jachin.*

Q. How high was the Door of the Middle Chamber?
A. So high that a Cowan could not reach to stick a Pin in.
Q. whcn you came to the Middle what did you see?
A. The Resemblance of the Letter G.
Q. what did that G. denote?
A. One that's greater than you?
Q. Who's greater than I, that am a Free and Accepted Mason, the Master of a lodge?
A. The Grand Architect and Contriver of the Universe, or he that was taken up to the Top of the Pinnacle of the Holy Temple.
Q. Can you repeat the letter G?
A. I'll do my Endeavour.

The repeating the Letter G.

Resp. In the Midst of *Solomon's* Temple there stands a G.
A Letter for all to read and see;
But few there be that understand
What means the Letter G.
Ex. My Friend, if you pretend to be
Of this Fraternity,
You can forthwith and rightly tell
What means that Letter G.
Resp. By Sciences are brought to Light

---

[206] Pair of Stairs – P. S. *patres societatis.*
[207] Three things – Three vows.

Bodies of various Kinds,
Which do appear to perfect Sight:
But none but Males shall know my Mind.
Ex. The Right shall.
Resp. If worshipful.
Ex. Both Right and Worshipful I am,
To hail you I have Command,
That you forthwith let me know,
As I you may understand.
Resp. By Letters Four and Science Five,[208]
This G aright doth stand,
In a due Art and Proportion;
You have your Answer, Friend.

N. B. Four Letters are Boaz; *Fifth Science Geometry.*

Ex. My Friend, you answer well,
If Right and Free Principles you discover,
I'll change your Name from Friend
And henceforth call you Brother.
Resp. The Sciences are well composed
Of noble Structure's Verse,
A Point, a Line, and an Outside;
But a Solid is the last.
Ex. God's good Greeting be to this our happy Meeting.
Resp. And all the Right Worshipful Brothers and Fellows.
Ex. Of the Right Worshipful and Holy lodge of St. *John's.*
Resp. From whence I came.
Ex. Greet you, greet you, greet you thrice heartily well, craving your Name.
Resp. *Timothy Ridicule.*[209]
Ex. Welcome, Brother, by the Grace of God.

N. B. *The Reason they denominate themselves of the Holy lodge of St. John's is, because he was the forth runner of our Savior, and laid the first parallel Line to the Gospel. Others do assert, that our Savior himself was*

---

[208] Science Five – This expression is not used in English or French; it is a barbarism. What is meant here is the science of the five virtues, recommended by Saint Ignatius.

[209] Timothy Ridicule – T. 19 R 17; making 36. The numbers 3 and 6 give the number 9 or the letter I. The Jesuits call a Mason Timothy Ridicule, and find this pleasant.

accepted a Free Mason whilst he was in the Flesh;[210] but how ridiculous and prophane it seems; I leave to the judicious Reader to consider.

The End of the Fellow Craft's Part.

---

[210] Our Saviour a Free-Mason, whilst he was in the Flesh – Prichard speaks here as something ridicule what a member of the Kilwinning Society had carved allegorically as a precious truth of Masonry. These poor carvings were rather expense in 1786. Jesus was represented in them as child on the laps of the mother, greeting his dear friend John, Freemason, and giving him a Templar star. I cannot remember how many points it had, but since I saw at least thirty copies of these sold during the same meeting, it will be possible to find soon these very precious prints.

The Master's Degree

Q. Are you a Master Mason?
A.. I am; try me, prove me, disprove me if you can.
Q. Where was you passed Master?
A. In a perfect lodge of Masters.
Q. What makes a perfect lodge of Masters?
A. Three.
Q. How came you to be passed Master?
A. By the Help of God, the Square, and my own Industry.
Q. How was you passed Master?
A. From the Square to the Compass.
Ex. An Enterd' Prentice I presume you have been.
R. *Jachin* and *Boaz* I have seen;
A Master-Mason I was most rare,
With Diamond, Ashler, and the Square.
Ex. If a Master-Mason you would be,
You must rightly understand the Rule of Three.
And M. B. [Mac-Benah.] shall make you free:[211]
And what you want in Masonry,
Shall in this lodge be shewn to thee.
R. Good Masonry I understand,
The Keys of all lodges are at my Command.[212]
Ex. You're an heroick Fellow; from whence came you?
R. From the East.
Ex. Where are you a-going?
R. To the West.
Ex. What are you going to do there?
R. To seek for that which was lost and is now found.
Ex. What was that which was lost and is now found?[213]
R. The Master Mason's Word.
Ex. How was it lost?
R. By three great Knocks, or the Death of our Master *Hiram*.

---

[211] M. B. Shall make you free – Which is to say Charles II once enthroned will make the Jesuits free and powerful in England, etc.

[212] Keys of all lodges are at my Command – The Master Mason represents the spiritual coadjutor who is the guide of Freemasons.

[213] Lost and found – The word lost and found. This is the sovereign word, the son of Charles I.

3. Masonry Dissected – Notes and Proofs

Ex. How came he by his Death?

R. In the Building of *Solomon's* Temple he was Master Mason, and at high 12 at Noon, when the Men were gone to refresh themselves, as were his usual Custom, he came to survey the Works; and when he was entered into the Temple, there were three Ruffians,[214] supposed to be three Fellow-Crafts, planted themselves at the three Entrances of the Temple; and when he came out, one demanded the Master's Word of him; and he replied, he did not receive it in such a Manner; but Time and a little Patience would bring him to it. He, not satisfied with that Answer, gave him a Blow which made him reel. He went to the other Gate; where he was accosted in the same Manner, and making the same Reply, he received a greater Blow, and at the Third his *Quietus*.

Ex. What did the Ruffians kill him with?

R. A Setting-Maul, Setting-Tool, and Setting-Beetle.

Ex. Carried him out at the West Door of the Temple, and hid him under some Rubbish till high 12 again.

Ex. What Time was that?

R. High 12 at Night, whilst the Men were at Rest.

Ex. How did they dispose of him afterwards?

R. They carried him up to the Brow of the Hill, where they made a decent Grave, and buried him.

Ex. When was he missed?

R. The same Day.

Ex. When was he found?

R. Fifteen Days afterwards.[215]

Ex. Who found him?

R. Fifteen[216] loving Brothers, by Order of King *Solomon*, went out of the West Door of the Temple, and divided themselves from Right to Left, within Call of each other; and they agreed, that if they did not find the Word in him, or about him, the first Word should be the Master's Word. One of the Brothers, being more weary than the rest, sat down to rest himself; and taking hold of a Shrub, which came easily up, and perceiving the Ground to have been broken, he hailed his Brethren; and pursuing their Search, found him decently buried in a handsome Grave 6 Foot East, 6 West, and 6 foot perpendicular;[217] and his Covering was green Moss and Turf; which surprised them; whereupon they replied, *Muscus Domus Dei Gratia*; which,

---

[214] Three Knocks, three Fellows, three Ruffians – These three ruffians represent for the Jesuits the three kingdoms that expelled them impolitely.

[215] Fifteen days afterwards – This means that the good brothers impolitely expelled take refuge under the protection of their Jesuit fathers.

[216] Fifteen – 15 gives the letter I, which is to say patres. Ordo of King Salomon. – A new sign of the general of the Society.

[217] Six foot East, 6 foot West and six foot perpendicular – Three times six give eighteen or the letter S. This is again societas, the society where Hiram or the order focuses on reuniting its head to the trunk.

according to Masonry, is, *Thanks be to God, our Master has got a Mossy House*; So they covered him closely; and, as a farther Ornament, placed a Sprig of Cassia at the Head of his Grave, and went and acquainted King *Solomon*.

Ex. What did King *Solomon* say to all this?
R. He ordered him to be taken up and decently buried, and that 15 Fellow-Crafts, with white Gloves and Aprons,[218] should attend his Funeral ---. [*Which ought, among Masons, to be performed to this Day.*]
Ex. How was Hiram raised?
R. As all other Masons are, when they receive the Master's Word.
Ex. How is that?
R. By the Five Points of Fellowship.
Ex. What are they?
R. Hand to Hand (1), Foot to Foot (2); Cheek to Cheek (3), Knee to Knee (4), and Hand to Back (5).

N. B. *When Hiram was taken up, they took him by the Fore finger, and the Skin came off, which is called the Slip; the spreading the Right Hand, and placing the Middle Finger to the Wrist, clasping the Fore-finger, and the Fourth, to the Sides of the Wrist, is called the Gripe; and the Sign is, placing the Thumb of the Right Hand to the Left Breast, extending the Fingers.*

Ex. What's a Master Mason named?
R. *Cassia* is my Name, and from a just and perfect lodge I came.
Ex. Where was Hiram interred?
R. In the *Sanctum Sanctorum*.
Ex. How was he brought in?
R. At the West Door of the Temple.
Q. What are the Master Jewels?
it. The Porch, Dormer, and Square Pavement.
Q. Explain them.
R. The Porch, the Entering into the *Sanctum Sanctorum*, the Dormer the windows or Lights within, the Square Pavement the Ground Flooring.
Ex. Give me the Master's Word?
Q. Whispers[219] him in the Ear, and supported by the five Points of Fellowship before-mentioned, says *Mac-Benah*, which signifies, *The Builder is smitten*.

---

[218] Gloves and Aprons – They mean that the Jesuits, not daring showing their *angelic* faces anymore, hide under the Freemason attire. This is why they call the Masonic apron an attire, the attire of the order.
[219] Whispers – These whispers express the caution and measures of the Jesuits to not reveal themselves to Freemasons.

3. Masonry Dissected – Notes and Proofs

N. B.   *If any Working Masons*[220] *are at Work; and you have a Desire to distinguish Accepted Masons from the rest, take a Piece of Stone, and ask him what it smells of: He immediately replies, neither Brass, Iron, nor Steel,*[221] *but of a Mason; then by asking him how old he is, he replies, above Seven, which denotes he has passed Master.*

The End of the Master's Part.

END

---

[220] Working Masons – To distinguish them from the *Accepted Masons* or Ours. One must use a *piece of stone* to recognize a Mason, which is to say one must be a father of the society to recognize an Our.

[221] Brass Iron, Steel – B.I.S. This father must be from the Society of the Blessed Saint Ignatius, *beati Ignatii societas.*

Bibliography

The following bibliography includes both works referenced by Nicholas de Bonneville and those used in the verification and preparation of this translation. Many of the references given by de Bonneville cite works of the 16th century or earlier in French, German, English and Latin languages. I have tried to reconstitute these references here to facilitate the works of those interested.

- à Kempis. *De imitatione Christi*. 1418. Translated as *The Imitation of Christ* by Atkinson, William and Margaret Beaufort in 1502.
- Anderson, James. *The Constitutions of the Ancient and Honourable Fraternity of Free and Accepted Masons*. 1767. More commonly known as *Anderson's Constitutions of 1738*.
- Andreae, Johann Valentin. *Assertion*, 1614.
- Andreae, Johann Valentin. *La Fama*, 1614.
- Andreae, Johann Valentin. *Mythologia Christiana*. 1618. Translated as *Christian Mythology*. 1618.
- Anonymous. *Entretiens sur les Voyages de Cyrus*. 1728. See Ramsey.
- Anonymous. *Jachin and Boaz; or, An Authentic Key to the Door of Free-Masonry, Both Ancient and Modern*. London, 1797.
- Anonymous. *Le tuileur-expert*. Paris, 1828
- Anonymous. *Royal Art of the Rose Croix Knight*. London. 1770.
- Anonymous. *Ueber den Zweck des Freymaurerordens*. Berlin, 1778. Possibly *Ueber den Zweck des Ordens der Frey-Maurer*.
- Anton, Carl Gottlob von. *Untersuchung uber das Gehemniss und die Gebrauche der Tempelherren {An Inquiry into the Mystery and Usages of the Knights Templar}*, 1782.
- Anton, Carl Gottlob von. *Versuch einer Geschichte des Tempelherren ordens {An Essay on the Order of Knights Templar}*, 1779. Translated into French as *Essai sur l'histoire de l'Ordre des Templiers*, 1840, by E. Fraissient.
- Aubineau, Léon. *Notices littéraires sur le dix-septième siècle*. Paris, 1859.
- Bacon, Francis. *Nova Atlantis*. 1624 . New Atlantis. 1627.
- Bacon, Francis. *Novum Organum*. 1620. Translated by J. Spedding as *The New Organon* in 1863.
- Bacon, Francis. *The Wisdom of the Ancients*. 1619.
- Barbier, Antoine-Alexandre. *Dictionnaire des ouvrages anonymes et pseudonymes*. Paris, 1823.
- Barruel, Augustin. *Memoirs illustrating the history of Jacobinism*. Volume 4. 1799.
- Bazot, Etienne François. *Manuel du franc-maçon*. Paris, 1817.
- Bésuchet, Jean-Claude. *Précis historique de l'ordre de la Franc-Maçonnerie depuis son introduction en France jusqu'en 1829*. Paris, 1829.
- Billington, James Hadley. *Fire in the Minds of Men: Origins of the Revolutionary Faith*. Basic Books, 1980.
- *Biographia Britannica*, 7 vols. London, 1747-63.
- Birkholz, Adam Michael. *Compass der Weisen*. Translated as *Compass of the Wise*. 1799. Authorship under the pseudonym Ketmia Vere alias Plumenoeck.
- Blackwell, Thomas. *Letters Concerning Mythology*. 1748. Translated into French by Marc-Antoine Eidous as *Lettres sur la mythologie*. Paris, 1771.
- Bloomfield, Samuel Thomas. Translation of *The History of Thucydides*, 1829.

Bibliography

- Boccaccio, Giovanni. *Decameron*. 1350-1353. Translated by John Florio (1620) and JM Rigg (1903).
- Bonnet, Charles. *Contemplation de la nature*. Amsterdam, 1764-1765. Translated by Bonnet as *The contemplation of nature*. London: printed for T. Longman, T. Becket and P. A. de Hondt, 1766.
- Bonneville, Nicholas de. *Histoire de l'Europe moderne : depuis l'irruption des peuples du Nord dans l'empire Romain, jusqu'à la paix de 1783 {History of Modern Europe: From the Invasion of Northern Peoples in the Roman Empire until the Peace of 1783}*. Paris; Geneva, 1789-1792. 3 Volumes.
- Bonneville, Nicholas de. *La maçonnerie écossaise*. Nîmes: C. Lacour. 1788, 1998. Translated by Eric Serejski as *Scottish Masonry*. 2011.
- Bonneville, Nicholas de. *Les Jésuites chassés de la maçonnerie, et leur poignard brisé par les maçons*. Paris, C. Volland. 1788 Translated by Eric Serejski as *Jesuits Driven Away from Masonry, and Their Dagger Shattered by the Masons*. 2011.
- Boulanger, Nicolas Antoine. *Le Christianisme dévoilé, ou Examen des principes et des effets de la religion chrétienne*. 1766. Translated by WM Johnson as *Christianity Unveiled*. 1835.
- Brou, Alexandre. *Les Jésuites de la légende*. Paris, 1907.
- Chappron, E. J. *Nécessaire maçonnique*. Paris, 5812 (1821).
- Chifflet, Jean-Jacques. *Anastasis Childerici I. Francorum Regis, sive Thesaurus Sepulchralis Tornaci Neruiorum ... (The Resurrection of Childeric the First, King of the Franks, or the Funerary Treasure of Tournai)*. 1655.
- Christie, Thomas. *The Analytical review, or History of literature, domestic and foreign on an enlarged plan*. 1794.
- Christophe, Jean Baptiste. *Histoire de la Papauté pendant le XIVe siècle avec des notes et des pièces justificatives*. Paris, .
- Cicero, Marcus Tullius. *De Natura Deorum*. 45 BC. Translated by Francis Brooks as *On the Nature of the Gods*. 1896.
- Coustos, John. *Procédures curieuses de l'Inquisition de Portugal contre les Francs-Maçons*. 1803.
- Cranz AF, von Starck JA, von Ditturth FD. *Stein des Anstosses und Fels der Aergerniss, allen meinen teutschen Mitbiirgern*. Gebruckt, 1780.
- D'Holbach, Paul-Henri Thiry. *Antiquité dévoilée par ses usages {Antiquity Unveiled through its Customs}*, 1766. Not to be confused with Robets' *Antiquity Unveiled*, 1892.
- D'Holbach, Paul-Henri Thiry. *Christianisme dévoilé*, 1761. Translated as *Christianity Unveiled* by W.M. Johnson, 1795 and as *Christianity Unveiled by Baron d'Holbach – A Controversy in Documents (Rescued from Obscurity)* by D.M. Holohan, 2008.
- de Loos, Onesime-Henri. *La Diadème des Sages, ou démonstration de la Nature inférieure; dans lequel on trouvera une analyse raisonnée du livre des Erreurs et de la Vérité*. Paris 1781.
- Dee, John. *Monas Hieroglyphica*, 1569.
- *Des droits du clergé dans les affaires publiques*, 1780.
- Draffen, George. *Some Further Notes on the Rite of Seven Degrees in London*. Ars Quatuor Coronatorum 68, 1956.
- Dupuy, Pierre. *Traittez concernant l'histoire de France; sçavoir la condamnation des Templiers, avec quelques actes; l'histoire du Schisme, les papes tenans le siege in Avignon; et quelques procez criminels*. Paris, 1654.

- Espiard de la Borde, Francois-Ignace. *Essais sur le génie et le caractère des nations* (printed later as *L'esprit des nations*). 1743. Translated as *The spirit of nations.* 1753.
- Favre, François. *Documents maçonniques recueillis et annotés.* Paris, 1866.
- Fénelon, François. *Les aventures de Télémaque.* 1699. Translated by Hawkesworth as *Adventures of Telemachus.* 1887.
- Fludd, Robert. *Summum Bonum.* Frankfurt, 1629.
- Fraissinet, Édouard. *Essai sur l'histoire de l'Ordre des Templiers.* Leipzig, 1779; Bruxelles, 1840.
- Gibbon, Edward. *The History of the Decline and Fall of the Roman Empire.* 1776
- Gloede, Herman. *Die Ordenswissenschaft entwickelt an dem Lehrlingsteppich.* Berlin, 1900.
- Goyder, David George. *Lectures on Freemasonry, Exhibiting the Beauties of the Royal Art.* London, 1864.
- Hall, Manly Palmer. *Collection of Alchemical Manuscripts*, 1500-1825 (1600). Archive.org
- Hammer, Joseph de. *Mémoire sur deux coffrets gnostiques du Moyen Age.* Paris, 1832.
- Hammond, Nicholas. *Fragmentary voices: memory and education at Port-Royal.* Tübingen : Narr, 2004.
- Harenberg , Johann Christoph. *Pragmatische Geschichte des Ordens der Jesuiten.* Halle-Helmstadt: Hemmerle, 1760.
- *Histoire, obligations et statuts de la très vénérable confraternité des Francs-Maçons.* Francfort sur le Mein, 1742.
- Homer. *The Iliad.* Murray and Butler translations (Online Perseus Project).
- Horace. *Epodes.* 30 BC. Translated with Comments by David Mankin. Cambridge, 1995.
- Hume, David. *Essays, Moral, Political, and Literary.* 1758.
- Hume, David. *The History of England.* 1754–62
- Hunt, Lynn; Jacob, Margaret C.; Mijnhardt, Wijnand. *The Book That Changed Europe: Picart and Bernard's Religious Ceremonies of the World.* Belknap Press of Harvard University, 2010.
- Irenaeus. *Against Heresies.* C. 180.
- Jannet, Claudio. *Les précurseurs de la franc-maçonnerie au XVIe et au XVIIe siècle.* Paris, 1887.
- Johannes Bolland, Johannes; de Tollenaer, Jean; and others. *Imago primi saeculi Societatis Iesu a Provincia Flandro-Belgica eiusdem Societatis repraesentata* ... Antuerpiae: Ex officina Plantiniana Balthasaris Moreti (*Image of the First Century of the Society of Jesus* also called *Jesuit Emblems from the Southern Netherlands*, refered to in this work as The *Imago Primi Soeculi*) . 1640.
- Jones, David. *The Secret History of White-Hall, From the Restoration of Charles II Down to the Abdication of the Late K. James.* 1717.
- Käpeen, Karl Friedrich (Possibly). *Allerneuste Entdeckung der verborgensten Geheimisse der hohen Stuffen der Freimaurerei.* 1766. French translation by Bérage. *Les Plus Secrets Mystères des Hauts Grades de la Maçonnerie Dévoilés.* Partial translation into English by S. Brent Morris, 33° and Eric Serejski, 32° in *Freemasonry In Context: History, Ritual, Controversy.* Lexington Books, 2004.

Bibliography

- Kelly, Douglas, Busby, Keith and Lacy Norris. *Conjectures: medieval studies in honor of Douglas Kelly*. Amsterdam – Atlanta. 1994.
- Knigge, Adolph F. R. L. *Avertissement aux princes allemands, pour les mettre en garde contre l'esprit et le poignard des Jésuites {A Warning to the German Princes to guard against the spirit and dagger of the Jesuits}*
- Knigge, Adolph F. R. L. *On The Jesuits, Freemasons and the German Rosicrucians*. 1781.
- Knigge, Adolph F. R. L. *Essay on Freemasonry*. 1784.
- Knigge, Adolph F. R. L. *Contribution towards the latest history of the Order of Freemasons*. 1786
- Krause, Karl Christian Friedrich. *Die drei ältesten Kunsturkunden der Freimaurerbrüderschaft*. 1820 {*The Three Oldest Professional Records of the Masonic Fraternity*}
- La Fontaine, Jean. *Fables*. 1668-1678.
- Lamberty, Guillaume de. *Memorial of the last England revolution containing the abdication of Jacques II, the advent of his majesty king Guillaume III to the crown and several other things arrived under his reign*. The Hague 1702.
- Lemaire, Jacques. *Les origines françaises de l'antimaçonnisme (1744-1797)* in Études sur le XVIIIè siècle, Éd. Université de Bruxelles, 1985.
- Lessing, Gotthold Ephraim. *Nathan der Weise*. 1778-1779. Translated by William Taylor as *Nathan the Wise*. 1893.
- Loen, Johann Michael von. *La véritable Religion, unique dans son espèce, universelle dans ses principes, corrompue par les disputes des théologies, divisée en plusieurs sectes, réunies en Christ*. Francfort, 1751.
- Loen, Johann Michael von. *Système de religion universelle*. 1753.
- Luchetti, Marco di. *Bonneville's Place in History*. 2009.
- Luther, Martin. *Libellus de instituendis pueris; magistratibus et senatoribus civitatum Germanioe*. 1521.
- Mackey, Albert Gallatin. *Encyclopedia of Freemasonry*. 1914.
- Maier, Michael. *Arcana arcanissima, hoc est, Hieroglyphica Ægyptio-Græca*. London: 1613.
- Maier, Michael. *Atalanta Fugiens*. 1617.
- Maier, Michael. *Symbola Aurea Mensoe*. 1614.
- Maier, Michael. *Thémis Auréa*. 1656.
- Marx, Karl; Engels, Friedrich. *Die Heilige Familie*. 1845. Translated as *The Holy Family*. 1956.
- Millot, Claude. *Elements of the History of England*. London: J. Johnson, 1771.
- Millot, Claude. *Elements of the History of France*. 1767-69.
- Milton, John. *Comus: a Mask*. 1637.
- Milton, John. *Paradise Regained*. 1671.
- Moegling, Daniel (alias Theophilus Schweighardt). *Speculum Sophicum Rhodo Stauroticum* {*Mirror of the Wisdom of the Rosicrucians*}. 1618.
- Montaigne, Michel de. *Essays*. 1575. Translated by Charles Cotton.
- Nicholson, Helen J. *Love, War and the Grail. Templars, Hospitallers and Teutonic Knights in Medieval Epic and Romance*. 1150-1500. 2001.
- Nicolaï, Christoph Friedrich. *Versuch über die Bersschuldigungen welch dem Tempelhermorden gemacht worden und über dessen Geheimniss; nebst einem Anhange uber das Entstehen der Freimaurergesellschaft* {*An Essay on the accusations made against the Order of Knights Templar and their mystery; with an Appendix on the origin of the Fraternity of Freemasons*}. Berlin. 1782.

- Oliver, George. *History of the Masonic Persecutions in Different Quarters of the Globe*. New York, 1867.
- Oliver, George. *The Golden Remains of the Early Masonic Writers*. London, 1847.
- Oliver, George. *The Historical Landmarks And Other Evidences Of Freemasonry Explained*. New York, 1855.
- Pascal, Blaise. *The Provincial Letters*. 1657.
- Pérau, Gabriel-Louis. *L'ordre des francs maçons trahi et Le secret des Mopses révélé*. Amsterdam. 1778.
- Peter, Émile. *L'égalité sociale ou les Jésuites et les Francs-Maçons dans le gouvernement des peoples depuis leur origine jusqu'à nos jours*. Paris, 1893
- Picart, Bernard. *Histoire des religions et des mœurs de tours les peuples du monde*. 1818. Volume 6 – Les Free-Massons.
- Preston, William. *Illustrations of Masonry*. London, 1829
- Prichard, Samuel. *Masonery Dissected*. 1730.
- Racine, Jean. *Esther*. Paris, 1689.
- Racine, Jean. *Iphigenia in Aulis*. 1674.
- Ramsey, Andrew Michael. *Les voyages de Cyrus, Avec un Discours Sur La Mythologie*. Paris, 1727. Translated as *The travels of Cyrus to which is annex'd a discourse upon the theology & mythology of the pagans*. London, 1728.
- Rasiel de Selva, Hercule (Quesnel, Pierre; de Plaix, César; Marchand, Prosper). *Histoire de l'admirable Dom Inigo de Guipuscoa [Ignacio de Loyola] chevalier de la Vierge : et fondateur de la monarchie des inighistes*. 1738. Anonym Translation from French into English as *History (the) of the wonderful Don Ignatius de Loyola, founder of the Order of the Jesuits; with an account of the establishment and government of that Order*. London, 1754.
- Rebold, Emanuel. *A General History of Free-Masons in Europe based upon the Ancient Documents relating to, and the Monuments erected by this Fratemity from its foundation in the Year 715 BC to the present time*. Cincinnati, 1869.
- Reed, David A. *How Semitic Was John? Rethinking the Hellenistic Background to John 1:1*. Anglican Theological Review, Fall 2003.
- Ribadeneira, Father. *Lives of the Saints,* probably *Flos Sanctorum*.
- Ribera, Francisco de. *De Templo Hierosolymitano et iis, quae ad templum pertinent, libri V. Salamant*. 1591.
- Riesbeck, M. le Bardon de. *Travels of Baron of Riesbeck*, 3 Vol. Paris, 1783, at Buisson. Translated by P.H. Maty as *Travels through Germany, in a series of letters*, 1787. French translation from English by Le Tourneur, *Voyage en Allemagne, dans une suite de lettres*. 1787.
- Roberts, Jonathan M. *Antiquity Unveiled*, 1892. Not to be confused with D'Holbach's *Antiquity Unveiled through its Customs}*, 1766.
- Rostaing, Léon. *Les anciennes loges maçonniques d'Annonay et les clubs*, 1766-1815. Lyon, 1903.
- Rousseau, Jean-Jacques. *Le Contrat Social*. 1763 or 1764. Translated by GDH Cole as *The Social Contract*.
- Saint Augustine. *De Genesi contra Manichaeos*. *On Genesis: A Refutation of the Manichees*. 401–415 C.E.
- Saint-Martin, Louis-Claude of. *Des Erreurs et de la Vérité {Of Errors and Truth}*. 1775.
- Saint-Martin, Louis-Claude of. *Discours sur la meilleure manière de rappeler à la raison les nations livrées aux erreurs et aux superstitions*. 1783.

Bibliography

- Saint-Martin, Louis-Claude of. Ode/Stances sur l'origine et la destination de l'homme . 1781/96.
- Saint-Martin, Louis-Claude of. *Tableau naturel des rapports qui existent entre Dieu, l'homme et l'univers.* 1782.
- Saint-Victor, Louis Guillemain de. *Recueil précieux de la maçonnerie Adonhiramite.* 1803.
- Smith, George. *The Use and Abuse of Free-Masonry.* London, Kearfley, 1783, New York: Masonic Publishing and Manufacturing Co. 1866.
- Smith, W. *A Dictionary of Christian biography, literature, sects and doctrines.* 1877.
- Sophocles, *Oedipus-king.*
- Starck, Johan. *Alte und neue Mysterien.* Berlin. 1782.
- Steinmetz, Andrew. *History of the Jesuits: from the foundation of their society to its suppression by Pope Clement XIV.* 1848.
- Studion, Simon. *Naometria, or Mercury of the Vessel, Measure of the Temple.* Sometimes attributed to John Dee.
- The English Review. No. IX. London, 1846. *Institutum SOcietatis Jesu.*
- The Freemasons Quarterly Magazine. Vol. 1. London, 1853. *Symbols and Symbolism.*
- The Republican. Volume XII. London, 1825. *Sixteen documents on Freemasonry.*
- Thou (Thuanus), Jacques Auguste de. *Historia sui temporis*, translated as *Histoire universelle*, Fr. trans. by C. le Beau, Le Mascrier, Des Fontaines, 1734.
- Tschudi, Théodore-Henri de; Bardou-Duhamel, Charles-Louis. *L'étoile flamboyante, ou La société des francs-maçons, considéré sous tous les aspects aspects.* Frankfurt, 1769.
- Typot, Jacob (or Typoest, Jacques, or Tipotius, Jacobus). *Symbola divina et humana pontificum imperatorum regum. Accessit brevis, et facilis isagoge.* 1601. Sometimes referred to as *Typotii emblemata.*
- Vinifauf or Vinsauf. *Itinerarium Regis Ricardi.* Translated as *Vinifauf's account of the expedition of King Richard I to the Holy-Land.* His authorship of this work appears to be false.
- Virgil. *The Aeneid.* 29–19 BCE
- Voltaire. Translated in English by Thomas Nugent as *An Essay On Universal History, The Manners, And Spirit Of Nations.* 1756.
- Voltaire. *Questions sur l'Encyclopédie.* 1770
- Waite, Arthur Edward, *A New Encyclopaedia of Freemasonry*, 1921,
- Ward, Henry Dana. *Free masonry. Its pretentions exposed in faithful extracts of its standard authors; with a review of Town's speculative Masonry.* New-York, 1828.
- Weidner, Johann Leonard. *Jubileum sive Speculum Jesuiticum, exhibens praecipua Iesuitarum scelera, molitiones, innovationes, fraudes, imposturas, & mendacia, contra statum ecclesiasticum, politicumque, in & extra Europaeum orbem, primo hoc centenario confirmati illius ordinis, instituta, & perpetrata; ex variis historiis, inprimis verò pontificiis collecta; cum mantissis aliquot & indice rerum; operâ & studio I.L.W.O.P..* 1643.
- Yarker, John. *The Arcane Schools: A Review of Their Origin & Antiquity with a General History of Freemasonry.* Belfast. 1909.
- Zaccone, Pierre. *Histoire de l'Inquisition des Jésuites et des Francs-maçons.* Paris, 1852.

www.ingramcontent.com/pod-product-compliance
Lightning Source LLC
Chambersburg PA
CBHW031204270326
41931CB00006B/397